Better Homes and Gardens®

GARDENING TIPS

100's of Tips, Techniques, and Ideas

from America's Gardening Experts

BETTER HOMES AND GARDENS® BOOKS

Des Moines

All of us at Better Homes and Gardens® Books are dedicated to providing you with the information and ideas you need to garden successfully. We guarantee your satisfaction with this book for as long as you own it. If you have any questions, comments, or suggestions, please write to us at:

MEREDITH® BOOKS
Gardening Books
Editorial Department, RW 240
1716 Locust St.
Des Moines, IA 50309-3023

BETTER HOMES AND GARDENS® BOOKS
An Imprint of Meredith® Books

GARDENING TIPS
Senior Editor: Marsha Jahns
Writers: Debra D. Felton, Karen Weir Jimerson
Associate Art Director: Tom Wegner
Designer: Lyne Neymeyer
Copy Editor: Mary Helen Schiltz
Production Manager: Douglas Johnston

Director, New Product Development: Ray Wolf
Managing Editor: Christopher Cavanaugh

Meredith Publishing Group
President, Publishing Group: Christopher Little
Vice President and Publishing Director: John P. Loughlin

Meredith Corporation
Chairman of the Board and Chief Executive Officer: Jack D. Rehm
President and Chief Operating Officer: William T. Kerr

Chairman of the Executive Committee: E. T. Meredith III

Quotations used throughout this book were taken from **Writings of the Plain Dirt Gardener** by Harry R. O'Brien, who was garden editor of *Better Homes and Gardens®* magazine years ago. A diary of his gardening experiences, **Writings of the Plain Dirt Gardener** was published in 1934.

We've compiled some of the best advice on all kinds of gardening from the people you trust the most: the experts at Better Homes and Gardens. From gardening basics to more advanced techniques, you'll find years of experience and wisdom on each and every page.

THE SUCCESSFUL GARDEN

"That time of year is at hand when our garden dreams begin to come true, when the long months of anticipation are over and our plans are consummated. The new things we bought or grew from seed are giving their first bloom."

Writings of the Plain Dirt Gardener

The Good Earth

- **Test your soil.** Before you spade or dig your garden in the spring, see if the soil is workable. Take one spadeful of soil, digging down at least 6 inches. Then pick up a handful and squeeze. If it's too wet to work, it will remain in a lump after you open your hand. If the soil crumbles when you open your hand, you can go ahead and dig.

- **Make it better.** To improve your soil, spade in plenty of organic matter before planting. It will pay low-maintenance dividends. Nutrient-rich sources include decomposed leaves, compost, grass clippings, and manure. Peat moss will help soil absorb and retain moisture.

- **Get it for less.** For bargains on soil, check with local gardening organizations. Community greenhouse groups often prepare and bag fine-quality potting soil to sell to the public at low cost.

- **Lighten the load.** To save on soil and to make extra-large pots and tubs lighter, fill the bottom with crumpled black-and-white newspaper and/or perlite, and top off with soil. If your plants are shallow rooted, you need only 6 to 8 inches of soil, even in a large pot.

- **Keep it moist.** Superabsorbent polymers are added to potting mixes or garden soil to help retain water. The polymers absorb hundreds of times their weight in water and give plants a source of moisture even after the soil itself dries out. This means you water less often. The polymers also hold dissolved nutrients, so fertilizers needn't be replenished as frequently. Polymer products are available at many nurseries. Mix the polymers with water and add them to your potting mix in the proportion recommended by the manufacturer.

What Is pH?

The pH scale is used to measure the relative acidity and alkalinity of the soil. It ranges from 0 to 14, with 7 indicating soil that is neutral. Soils with a pH less than 7 are acid; those above pH 7 are alkaline.

The pH balance of soil varies by region of the country and type of terrain. For example, swamps and bogs have a high percentage of peat and are very acidic. In humid regions, including most forests, the soil is moderately acid to slightly alkaline. Arid regions range from moderate to strongly alkaline.

Because of these differences, it is important to test your soil pH. Most garden centers stock an inexpensive pH tape that changes color to indicate the degree of acidity.

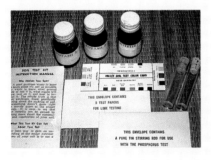

Testing Leftover Seeds

To test the vitality of leftover seeds, place a few on a wet paper towel and keep them moist. If the seeds sprout after the proper time, go ahead and plant them. If you get less than 50 percent germination, buy new.

BETTER GERMINATION

Many seeds require special conditions to nudge them out of dormancy and induce germination. One technique, called scarification, involves simply breaking or softening the hard outer coating of the seed so that it will germinate more quickly. Large seeds can be nicked with a sharp knife or file, or rubbed with sandpaper. Shake small seeds in a sandpaper-lined jar.

Another technique, called stratification, is used for plants from cold climates. Put the seeds between layers of moistened vermiculite or sand and peat either in a sealed jar or plastic bag. Store them in the refrigerator until they sprout.

SOWING SMALL SEEDS

If you find handling very small seeds frustrating (A million begonia seeds weigh just an ounce!), try one of these simple solutions.

- Put the seeds in an old salt shaker with a small amount of sand and sprinkle them on the soil mix.

- Mix the seeds with white table sugar or fine sand and then stir to distribute the seeds evenly. Use a spoon to spread the mixture over the planting medium. The sugar or sand will not harm the seeds.

- Run a strip of toilet paper down the furrow and plant the seeds on top. That way, you can see exactly where each seed is, and the buried paper will quickly break down into the soil.

Early Detection

- During the summer months, inspect your plants for insect or disease invasions and promptly remove any affected material. In addition to making your garden more attractive, prompt removal of damaged leaves and shoots cuts down on future cleanup chores by providing less opportunity for fungal and viral diseases to settle in and spread.

- To keep weeding chores from becoming overwhelming, try to spend just 10 minutes a day weeding the garden. You'll be surprised how pulling only a few weeds each day will enable you to keep them from getting out of hand. Being in the garden on a daily basis will also let you spot pest and disease problems while they are minor and easy to manage.

CONTROL THOSE PESTS

- Not every creeping, crawling creature is a pest. Predatory insects, such as ladybugs, praying mantises, and lacewings, keep bad bugs at bay.

- Save money by applying pest controls at the right time. For instance, don't spray when it is raining or windy or when the sun is bright. You'll waste both effort and the cost of the spray, because you will soon have to repeat the procedure.

- Hand-picking slugs, beetles, and tomato or cabbage worms costs nothing. Knock these and other similar creatures off the plant with a strong blast of water from a hose. Or, brush them off into a can of soapy water.

- Have a water source, such as a birdbath or water-filled crock, in or near the garden to attract insect-eating birds.

Disease Prevention

- When you see the word "resistance" applied to a plant, it means that it can ward off attacks by certain insects or diseases. A resistant variety is less likely than a nonresistant variety to contract the disease or be attacked by the pest to which it is resistant. A tolerant variety is not particularly resistant to the pest or disease organism, but it is better able to withstand the damage and continue growing than a nontolerant variety.

- Massed plantings can be a disaster when the group is devastated by rampaging diseases. If you want to include a large cluster of the same plant in your garden, choose an extra-tough variety that resists diseases.

- If you are unsure if a plant is suitable for your garden, just plant one or two specimens initially. If they survive and flourish, continue to add more.

- To prevent damping-off disease, a disease that can kill a whole pot of seedlings in just a day or two, use sterilized soil and provide space for air to circulate between seedlings. Or use sphagnum moss instead of soil for covering seeds. After sowing seeds on top of the moist potting medium, sprinkle a thin layer of finely milled sphagnum moss over the top. Pat lightly and mist thoroughly with room-temperature water to moisten.

- Choose native plants and wildflowers, such as black-eyed Susan (*Rudbeckia hirta*), shown below. Plants that are indigenous to your region are accustomed to the climate and soil type. They're also more naturally immune to pests and diseases.

Finicky Eaters

➤ If deer are hungry enough, they will eat practically anything. However, gardeners report that deer do not like the following plants: monkshood (*Aconitum* spp.), baneberry (*Actae* spp.), flowering onion (*Allium* spp.), lily-of-the-valley (*Convallaria majalis*), foxglove (*Digitalis* spp.), and daffodil (*Narcissus* spp.). Deer also tend to avoid prickly, spiny plants.

➤ Some plants are reputed to be a good defense against harmful insects. Marigolds, for example, are said to effectively deter some types of garden insects.

➤ In general, slugs do not like to chew on the following plants: *Astilbe* spp. (shown above), hardy begonia (*Begonia grandis*), wild bleeding-heart (*Dicentra eximia*), foxglove (*Digitalis* spp.), *Epimedium* spp., Lenten rose (*Helleborus orientalis*), impatiens cultivars, and Jacob's-ladder (*Polemonium caeruleum*).

TOOLS AND EQUIPMENT

Secondhand Tools

Garage sales are an excellent source of gardening tools at low prices. Select tools that have been well maintained, then give them a thorough cleaning. Use steel wool to shine metal parts, and clean up wooden handles with a light sanding, followed by a coat of oil.

Safe Mower Repair

Before you work on any power mower, disconnect the spark-plug wire to avoid an accidental ignition. If you tilt the mower to examine the underside, do not do it over grass or near other plantings, which could be damaged by a gasoline spill.

Protective Knee Pads

Gardeners spend a lot of time on their knees. Use a purchased kneeler or improvise one by placing a piece of foam rubber in a plastic bag.

Photographic Memories

To help remember what plants you planted where, take photographs throughout the seasons. The photo record also will be useful for future landscape changes.

Low-Cost Lights

Special grow lights cost more money than fluorescent ones, yet recent research indicates plants grow well under either. Save even more by finding fluorescent fixtures on sale.

Clog-Free Sprayers

Always strain a homemade spray several times through cheesecloth or very fine screening. If you don't, the solution may clog the sprayer.

Heavy-Duty Pots

Plastic pots are convenient to use and store, but they are light in weight and are apt to blow over in strong wind. When you plant in plastic pots, either put them inside larger, more decorative pots or add stones to the bottom to give added weight.

Quick Fix for Cut Flowers

Some cut flowers—notably poppies (shown above), tithonias, hollyhocks, hibiscus, dahlias, oleanders, and snow-on-the-mountain—bleed sap when they're cut. Before arranging them in a vase, seal the stems by quickly passing the cut ends over an open flame.

Gardening Support

To get the most from your gardening experience. . .

• Join a garden club. You'll gather information and advice— and maybe even share plants with other gardeners.

• Consider starting a plant fundraiser. Ask members of an organization you support to grow and nurture a few flats of flowers or vegetables, then donate them to the sale.

Container Cleanup

Keeping flowerpots clean helps prevent plant disease. In the cool days of autumn, scrub the pots that held your annual container gardens, then carefully store them for another season.

• To remove salt and clinging earth from clay pots, rub them with steel wool and diluted vinegar, then soak them in a bleach solution.

• Clean plastic pots with a cloth dipped in warm, soapy water. Scrub the pots until they're free of soil and grime, then soak them in a bleach solution.

Water Wisdom

- Your garden's need for water will vary according to the type of plant, the temperature of the air, and the velocity of the wind (high winds speed evaporation). Also, shallow-rooted plants need more water than those with deep roots.

- Overhead sprinklers are the least efficient way to water because much of the water evaporates in hot sun or warm air or is blown away by winds. Trickle or drip systems that supply water directly to the root zone are best. Drip systems use plastic or rubber tubing with tiny holes that allow water to seep slowly into the soil.

- Save time and conserve water by grouping plants in your garden by their similar moisture needs: water guzzlers (plants that need a lot of supplementary water), moderate drinkers (plants that need supplementary water during dry spells), and drought-tolerant species (plants that need little or no supplementary water once they're established).

- To conserve, water your garden during the cool, calm hours of early morning.

Wet 'n' Wild

- If your growing area is extremely wet in only one small place, a concentrated soil amendment job may quickly solve the problem. Dig a deep hole—as much as 2 feet deep—and fill it with a blended mixture of half the original dirt and half compost and other organic matter.

- If you invest in a water system for your yard, install it in sections over several years to avoid a heavy expense in any one year.

- If you garden in a part of the country that is subject to heavy rains, cover newly seeded areas with one of the new lightweight floating row covers or "garden blankets" that allow light and air to penetrate but prevent heavy raindrops from dislodging the soil and disturbing seeds.

Drought Defiers

Select drought-defying plants to beat the summer heat. Along with desert species, you can count on a variety of perennials and annuals to thrive in dry soil.

The phrase "tolerates dry soil" is one clue to look for. Heat-resistant annuals include zinnia, portulaca, gaillardia, ageratum, and petunia (shown at right). For a more tropical look, use banana, elephant's-ear, castor bean, canna lily, caladium, coleus, and rice-paper plant. For sunny places, plant bamboo, yucca, agave, Chinese hibiscus, lantana, and pampas grass.

ROOM TO GROW

When you decide on a spot for your garden, place it in a location where you can expand it in the future, if you desire.

MUCH ADO ABOUT MULCH

Mulch discourages weeds, returns nutrients to the soil, and protects plants during cold winter months. Many materials can be used to help your garden get the most out of mulch.

- To reduce evaporation and runoff, mulch around plants with a 3- to 4-inch layer of organic material, such as shredded bark, pine needles, grass clippings, or straw.

- Rake tree leaves into a pile, use the lawn mower to shred them, then spread a thick layer in part of the garden. Earthworms will enjoy the leaves all winter, and you can use them for mulch in the spring.

- Don't put grass clippings on the garden until they dry for a day or two. Clippings tend to heat up so much when they first begin to decompose that they can actually damage plant parts.

- When you get material from a brush-cutting operation, ask what you are getting. It may not be as attractive as you want. During summer months, for instance, it may contain green leaves and larger twigs, depending on the size of the chipper used.

- Golf courses generate a lot of grass clippings. Ask to take some for your garden or compost pile.

- For extra protection in winter, add an inch or two of mulch on top of what's already in your garden. If winter winds blow some of your mulch off the garden, replace it as soon as you can. If necessary, cover the mulch with boards or tarps to keep it in place.

- Be creative with mulches. Use different ones in different places. Consider mixing two kinds for a unique look.

Low-Maintenance Mulch

For wood-product mulches and gravel, look in the telephone directory under Building Materials, Landscape Equipment and Supplies, Rock, or Stone.

- Wood mulches are sold in bags or in bulk. A 2-cubic-foot bag will cover an area of 8 square feet about 3 inches deep.
- When buying in bulk, estimate that 1 cubic yard will cover 108 square feet, about 3 inches deep.
- The amount of gravel needed varies somewhat with the size of the gravel, but generally a ton of rock covers 100 square feet.

7 STEPS TO QUALITY COMPOSTING

To turn refuse into rich organic matter and nutrients for your garden, start your own compost pile.

- Find a secluded, shady area on your property and build at least two composting enclosures out of wire, blocks, or planks. (If you construct two piles, material can be added to one while compost is forming in the other.) The size of these enclosures depends largely on your needs and the availability of refuse.

- Before you construct your enclosures, check with your local energy-conservation groups. They sometimes offer good-quality plastic compost bins for very little money.

- To make a compost pile, alternate layers of vegetation with soil, shredded leaves, or even sawdust. Add grass clippings only in thin layers, or they will mat down and start to smell.

- To collect kitchen waste for your compost pile, keep a plastic container by your sink and slip castoffs into the container. (Cut up large items, such as watermelon rinds.) At the end of the day, deposit the contents on the compost heap. Cover the kitchen waste with shredded leaves before adding the next layer.

- After the refuse in the compost enclosure reaches about 6 inches in depth, add a cup or two of limestone and cover it with an even 1-inch layer of soil. More refuse can then be layered on top of this until your soil sandwiches reach the top of the enclosure.

- Once a week or so, turn the pile with a pitchfork to allow decomposition to proceed at an even pace. If the weather is dry, you will need to water the pile occasionally to keep it moist. Compost is ready to use when it is dark brown, crumbly, and earthy smelling.

- If you turn your compost pile once a week and decomposition seems to be proceeding slowly, the ingredients may be too dry. A dry heap will not allow sufficient bacterial action to result in perfect compost. So if rainwater is not sufficient, you must occasionally add moisture. Spray the pile with a hose until the contents are as wet as a wrung-out sponge. Eventually the bacteria will break down the organic matter into a rich, dark brown humus that is completely free of odor but rich with benefits for your plants.

LANDSCAPING

Landscaping for Beginners

- **Gather ideas.** Visit public gardens throughout the year to get good plant ideas. You'll see firsthand what various plants look like, and you'll come away with plenty of ideas you can incorporate in your own garden design.

- **Keep your landscape plan simple.** It can be effective without being elaborate. Often an inviting path and some colorful plants are all you need.

- **Don't limit gardens to the backyard.** Put them out front as well. Whether your preferences run to flowers, herbs, vegetables, or ornamental grasses, use plants to create an inviting entrance.

- **Visualize your completed landscape.** Consider how things will look not just at the time the work is completed, but also in 5 years, 10 years, and 25 years. Consider, too, that your landscaping needs are probably going to change over time.

"I've come to see that gardening in the true sense means the whole home outside the house in which we live. It's the lawn, the trees, the shrubs—everything from the street to the rear line, not just the portion where we grow flowers in beds."

Writings of the Plain Dirt Gardener

SECRET GARDEN

Grow a Screen: Tall, slender trees and shrubs, such as tall hedge buckthorn, emerald arborvitae, bradford pear, columnar Norway maple, and skyrocket juniper, are perfect for exposed front entries or corner lots, where space and privacy are at a premium.

8 Easy Ways to Give Your Yard Pizzazz

Simple landscaping steps can mean the difference between a mediocre yard and a memorable one.

- Add an inviting path and line it with colorful plants.
- Choose plants that complement one another in height, bloom time, and color. Assign tall-growing plants to spots behind the medium-size plants. Save the front of the border for low-growing and creeping plants.
- Put one tall plant, three medium plants, and five short plants together. Plant the tall one slightly off center, group the medium plants together, then intersperse the small, ground-hugging plants among the others.
- Don't settle for the same old plants. Look around for something different. For example, substitute sweet woodruff for the ground cover pachysandra, and plant ornamental grasses in place of a traditional lawn.
- Take advantage of underused locations around your house, such as side yards, alleyways, slopes, and driveway edges.
- Dress up your yard with a flowering vine like clematis. It will cling to almost any surface, transforming a fence, porch pillar, arbor, or stairway railing into a bower of bloom. Other fast-growing flowering vines include trumpet vine, wisteria, jasmine, silverlace, honeysuckle, and Dutchman's pipe.
- Add architectural interest to your yard with containers. Terra-cotta pots, stone urns, and window boxes offer focal points—often where nothing else will grow—on decks and patios, along walkways, around a pool, hanging from awnings or latticework, and atop walls.
- Plant flowers in a raised bed. That way you can enjoy the fragrant blooms closer to nose level, and the plants will benefit from the enriched soil.

Dollars and Sense

- Tackle one area of your yard at a time. Divide a project to spread out the costs and the work. Before you know it, your lot will be completely transformed.

- Hire a landscape designer to develop a garden plan. It can save you money in the long run. Once you have a detailed drawing, you can follow through and do the work yourself.

- Look for inexpensive alternatives to your more costly landscaping projects, or reassess their importance.

- For an affordable yet immediately established look, use your plant budget to buy larger trees. Shrubs, which grow much faster, can be purchased in smaller sizes.

- Line a walkway with flowers. One or two flats of bedding plants are usually enough to do the trick.

Best Plants for

Best Plants for Warm Climates

Some of the following plants will not survive when temperatures drop below 5° F.

- Scarlet sage (*Salvia splendens*) is a perennial in the southern U.S. and an annual elsewhere. It has brilliant red flowers.
- Lily-of-the-Nile (*Agapanthus orientalis*) is a bulb whose blue or white flowers bloom in summer.
- Kiwi berry (*Actinidia chinensis*) is a handsome vine with fragrant flowers and edible fruit.
- Crape myrtle (*Lagerstroemia indica*) is a small native tree with lovely summer flowers in colors from whites to purples.
- Camellia (*Camellia japonica*), a small tree, has glossy dark green leaves and beautiful large flowers.
- California lilac (*Ceanothus* x *delilianus*), a hybrid shrub, has pale or deep blue flowers.
- White rock rose (*Cistus* x *hybridus*) is a bushy shrub with white flowers throughout summer.

Lily-of-the-Nile

Best Plants for Cool Climates

Many of these plants can survive winter temperatures as low as -40° F.

- Monkshood (*Aconitum napellus*) is a perennial with rich violet-blue flowers.
- Garden peony (*Paeonia lactiflora* 'Festiva Maxima'), a perennial, has fragrant, white, double flowers.
- Iceland poppy (*Papaver nudicaule*) is a perennial with fragrant flowers in many colors.
- Siberian squill (*Scilla siberica*) is a bulb with brilliant blue flowers in spring.
- Canada wild ginger (*Asarum canadense*), a ground cover, has green heart-shaped leaves.
- Chokecherry (*Prunus virginiana* 'Shubert') is a native tree with foliage that turns red in summer. It bears purple fruit used for making jelly.
- Siberian dogwood (*Cornus alba* 'Sibirica') is a native shrub with vivid coral red bark.
- Appalachian tea (*Viburnum cassinoides*) is a shrub with red fall foliage and multicolored berries.

Landscaping

Best Warm-Season Grasses

Plant warm-season grasses, such as hybrid Bermuda, St. Augustine, and zoysia, by using sprigs, stolons, or plugs or by sodding. Planting living pieces of grass is the only way to establish these grasses, because they don't set viable seed. Buy sprigs or plugs by mail or from a sod farm, following their advice on the quantity or order. When the plants arrive, be sure to store them in a shady spot, keep them moist, and plant them as soon as possible.

Best Insect-Resistant Grasses

Certain varieties of perennial ryegrass, turf-type tall fescues, and fine fescues live in a symbiotic relationship with a group of naturally occurring beneficial fungi called endophytes. These fungi produce toxins that repel insects such as chinch bugs, sod webworms, billbugs, armyworms, and aphids. You can introduce endophytes to the lawn only through seed, and the seed must be less than a year old to be effective. Check the label on the seed package to learn the age of the seed and whether endophytes are present.

Best Plants to Avoid

Attractive plants can soon become uncontrolled weeds when planted in good garden soil. Don't plant these unless you can find methods to confine them.

- Trumpet creeper (*Campsis radicans*), a vine, has bright red tubular flowers throughout summer.
- Oriental bittersweet (*Celastrus orbiculatus*) is a vine with bright yellow seedpods opening to reveal orange berries in fall. Plant the native species, *Celastrus scandens,* instead.
- Hardy ageratum (*Eupatorium coelestinum*) is a perennial with blue flowers in late summer.
- Gooseneck loosestrife (*Lysimachia clethroides*) is a perennial with white flowers throughout much of summer.
- Sundrops (*Oenothera fruticosa*), a perennial, has yellow flowers in late spring and early summer.
- Star-of-Bethlehem (*Ornithogalum umbellatum*) is a bulb with clusters of white flowers in spring.
- Flowering raspberry (*Rubus odoratus*), a shrub, has magenta flowers in summer.

Star-of-Bethlehem

Color and Shade

Although shade flowers generally fall into the pastel ranges, several plants have red, orange, or yellow blossoms.

- For red flowers, plant hardy fuchsia (*Fuchsia magellanica*), impatiens, cardinal flower (*Lobelia cardinalis*), and bee-balm (*Monarda didyma*).
- Oranges include tuberous begonia (shown below), Turk's-cap lily (*Lilium superbum*), and flame azalea (*Rhododendron calendulaceum*).
- To add yellow to your garden, plant lady's-mantel (*Alchemilla vulgaris*), Siberian pea tree (*Caragana arborescens*), golden star (*Chrysogonum virginianum*), and moneywort (*Lysimachia nummularia*).

Even the darkest areas of your yard are suitable for these plants.

- Shrubs include fatsia (*Fatsia japonica*), sweet box (*Sarcococca hookerana* var. *humilis*), and skimmia (*Skimmia japonica*).
- Good ground covers for shade are carpet bugleweed (*Ajuga reptans*), wild ginger (*Asarum* spp.), Kenilworth ivy (*Cymbalaria muralis*), and pachysandra.
- Other plants for shady spots include wall fern (*Polypodium vulgare*), annual impatiens, perennial bear's-breech (*Acanthus mollis*), and baneberry (*Actaea* spp.).

The Study of Path-ology

When you plan a garden path, look beyond the standard-issue concrete ribbon. Consider materials that enhance the environment, such as brick, stone, gravel, or even shredded bark. The shortest distance across the yard may be a straight path, but a path that curves and meanders offers more visual appeal.

Making a path

Take your time when working on a path. Don't expect to do it all in one day. Draw a plan on paper, then lay the path out in the yard with rope or hose before beginning to dig.

To create interest when building a path, pay attention to the interplay of the path's materials with the textures of the garden. In a dry wild garden, for example, try a riverlike path of crushed stones with larger stepping-stones within its boundaries.

Place black plastic underneath a path of white pebbles. The plastic will save you hours of weeding by smothering any plants that might try to emerge through the pebbles.

LIGHT SHOW

Lights can add beauty, safety, and security to your landscape. Use lighting to showcase a spectacular plant or garden feature, to set a romantic mood, to illuminate steps and walkways, and to flood remote areas of the yard.

Friendly Fences and Walls

- Fences and walls frame, accent, and provide background to set off plantings, such as *Salvia farinacea,* shown below. They unify a yard, and they keep kids and pets in and unwanted visitors out. Mix opaque and open styles to camouflage unsightly views and accent pleasing vistas. Use tall fences for privacy and short ones for accent.

- Good fences may make good neighbors, but standing alone, a fence view can be monotonous. Add excitement by planting flowering shrubs nearby for color and interest. Almost any species will do; just be sure to find out the mature size and shape of the shrub you choose. Dense, slow-growing shrubs such as azaleas and rhododendrons rarely grow out of bounds.

- Be sure to check local zoning ordinances to learn height restrictions for fencing. Some ordinances may allow only 6-foot or 8-foot fences.

Creative Camouflage

✤ *Use plants as screens to make a small space seem larger and a large one more intimate. They also can add a feeling of separation to outdoor rooms by breaking up the space.*

✤ *Cracking foundations, forlorn fences, woebegone walls, and other common landscape ailments can take time and money to repair. Until then, cure the problem with ground covers. Good choices for camouflaging problem areas include blooming heather, White Meidiland rose, winter creeper, rock cotoneaster, and creeping juniper.*

Giving Your Garden an Edge

Edging can serve a variety of purposes. Use it to. . .

- define the garden boundary.

- act as a frame, setting off whatever is planted inside.

- keep a garden path in its place.

- keep plants inside borders.

DECK OR PATIO?

All decked out. Decks allow you to gain outdoor living space on level, sloping, or hilly lots. To give a deck more appeal, round or angle at least one corner of the deck, vary the pattern or the levels of the deck, or surround it with interesting planters or plantings.

The pleasures of patios. A patio offers you almost endless possibilities—as an appealing entry, as an underused side-yard option, or as a backyard staple. Locate a patio for sun, shade, or wind protection, and make sure drainage is good. Use plants or railings for privacy and arbors or roofs for shade.

Slope Solutions

Turn the slope in your yard into a hardworking hillside by installing terraced beds. The beds not only provide a place to garden but also help prevent soil erosion. Create the terrace walls with stones, landscaping ties, or brick pavers, and then plant each terrace as a mini garden.

Mass plantings of spring-flowering bulbs, wildflowers, ornamental grasses, and quick-growing ground covers can protect a hillside from erosion. Gentle hillsides are perfect for apple and pear trees, grapes, and vegetables. Shrubs, especially interplanted with hedges, also do well.

JUST FOR KIDS

One of the best ways to introduce kids to nature and gardening is by creating an outdoor area just for them. The playground should have wide paths, a grassy play area in a sunny, well-drained spot, carefully outlined garden beds, at least one shady spot, and equipment such as swings and a sandbox.

FLOWERS FOR FALL COLOR

Your entire landscape can be as colorful as falling autumn leaves when you plant flowers with fall color in mind. Summer annuals such as 'Imagination' verbena, 'Mont Blanc' nierembergia, and Dahlberg daisy continue their vibrant show into early fall. Rely on perennials such as asters, rudbeckia, blue sage, or 'Autumn Joy' sedum, shown at left, to weave other brilliant hues into your fall garden.

Plan Before You Plant

Lay out gardens before you start digging. Use a hose to mark the curving shape for informal gardens. Trace the hose line with sand, then remove the hose for a nicely defined line. Follow the same technique, using string and stakes with sand, for formal, straight-lined beds and borders.

Choose the right plants. For best results, purchase only trees, shrubs, and perennials that are hardy to your region. If you garden in the North, avoid species that are described as tender or marginally hardy.

Save a Shrub

Redoing your landscape? Save existing

shrubs and incorporate them into your land-

scape plan. Old, scraggly specimens often

can be given new life with careful pruning.

Good Advice

■ For landscaping advice, check with your local nursery or garden center. Often, they will have a landscaper on staff who can help you with specific questions.

■ Always buy nursery stock from a reputable source and make sure that it comes with a guarantee.

PERENNIALS

"'April showers bring May flowers,' but it's October planting and work that brings both April and May flowers, and don't you forget it, even if days are nipping cold sometimes."

Writings of the Plain Dirt Gardener

Steps to Success

- When adding new perennials to your garden, look for those designated as Perennial Plant of the Year selections. These are flowers honored by the Perennial Plant Association for their beauty, their long season of interest, and their low-maintenance requirements. The selections are widely available at garden centers and through mail-order nurseries. Past winners have included 'Moonbeam' coreopsis and 'Purple Palace' heuchera.

- Another option is to start with only one or two plants to test their resistance to disease and insects in your area. If they don't survive, the loss will be seen in only a small section of your garden.

- If you're unsure which perennials will succeed in a special area, ask the experts in your local Master Gardener program. Under the auspices of county cooperative extension agents, these trained volunteers answer horticultural questions and give advice about local growing conditions at no charge to the public. You'll save time and money by planting only perennials that are suitable for your area.

The Kindest Cut

Cutting flowers for indoor arrangements is a pleasurable way to deadhead many perennials, including coreopsis (shown at right), feverfew, rose mallow, bee-balm, heliopsis, coralbells, veronicas, and stokesias. Harvest flowers in the evening; avoid cutting them in the strong midday sun. Early morning is the second best time to cut. Carry a pail with a few inches of water while you cut; put each stem cut into the water at once. Cut soft stems with a knife or sharp scissors that won't crush the stem, and use pruning snips for woody stems. Cut stems at a slant to maximize the water-absorbing surface and prevent a stem from standing flat against the bottom of the container. Cut stems a bit longer than you think you will need.

Water Safety

WELL-TIMED TRANSPLANTS

Planting time. The best time to plant perennials is on a cool, cloudy day. If it's warm and sunny, keep plant roots shaded and covered with layers of wet newspapers until you are ready to plant. Remember that your main goal in transplanting is to avoid shocking the plants.

Rites of spring. Many popular perennials can be transplanted into the garden in spring. Pansies, foxgloves, Canterbury bells, columbine, and Shasta daisies are all easily moved if they are not allowed to dry out while being dug. Mulch all new plantings to increase soil moisture and prevent weed competition.

Germs and viruses often strike plants through moisture on the foliage, so it's risky to use an overhead sprinkler to water a perennial garden . Besides unnecessarily drenching leaves, the water emitted by overhead sprinklers takes a long time to reach and then soak into the soil where it is needed. Instead of overhead sprinklers, use soaker hoses or other drip irrigation systems that deliver water directly to the roots.

Although it is best to thin deeply rooted or woody plants in early spring or late fall, shallow-rooted plants such as sundrops (Oenothera) and fern-leaf coreopsis can be thinned at any time of the year. If they have overgrown their bounds, yank them out of the garden.

Best Perennials

REGIONAL FAVORITES

Many regional natives also will shine in other parts of the country.

■ *West*—British Columbia wild ginger (*Asarum caudatum*), a ground cover for dry shade; a hybrid of coralbells (*Heuchera maxima* x *Heuchera sanguinea* 'Santa Ana Cardina'); Silver King artemisia (*Artemisia ludoviciana* var. *albula* 'Silver King'); and Mexican evening primrose (*Oenothera berlandieri*), which bears pink flowers in late spring.

■ *Midwest*—American columbine (*Aquilegia canadensis*), which has red and yellow spurred flowers in early spring, and prairie blazing-star (*Liatris pycnostachya*), with spikes of lavender-purple flowers.

■ *Southeast*—green-and-gold (*Chrysogonum virginianum*), with bright yellow flowers in early spring, and obedient plant (*Physotegia virginiana*), with handsome pink flowers in late summer.

■ *Northeast*—black snakeroot (*Cimicifuga racemosa*), which has elegant, soaring wands of white flowers in midsummer, and the colorful New York asters (*Aster novi-belgii*).

People's Choice

Perennials that are easy to grow and readily available at retail outlets across the country include:

❧ 'Sprite' astilbe (*Astilbe simplicifolia* 'Sprite'), a diminutive hybrid with glossy, dark green foliage and sprays of shell-pink flowers in midsummer shade gardens.

❧ 'Moonbeam' coreopsis (*Coreopsis verticillata* 'Moonbeam'), with disks of pale yellow flowers on light, airy foliage all summer in sunny settings.

❧ 'Palace Purple' heuchera (*Heuchera micrantha* 'Palace Purple'), a partial-shade plant with handsome purple foliage all season and tiny bluish-white flowers on wiry stalks in summer.

❧ Creeping phlox (*Phlox stolonifera*), an evergreen, matted, woodland native ground cover with pink, white, or blue flowers in spring.

❧ 'Sunny Border Blue' veronica (*Veronica longifolia* var. *spicata* 'Sunny Border Blue'), with spikes of rich, violet-blue flowers in sunny gardens throughout summer.

Artemisia

Prairie Blazing-Star

Best Old-Fashioned Perennials

Many perennials were grown in gardens two or more centuries ago and are just as delightful today.

❧ Red Valerian (*Centranthus ruber*) has red, pink, or white flowers throughout summer with good-looking grayish-blue foliage.

❧ Foxglove (*Digitalis purpurea*) has spires of pink to white flowers. Once a staple of medieval herb gardens, it is the source of the heart drug digitalis.

❧ Tawny daylily (*Hemerocallis fulva* 'Kwanso') is a common orange roadside flower. It's sturdy and easy to grow in all types of soil.

❧ Dame's rocket (*Hesperis matronalis*) is a fragrant, long-blooming perennial covered with lavender or white flowers. It's often naturalized at edges of wooded areas.

❧ Evergreen candytuft (*Iberis sempervirens*) is tidy and low growing, with sparkling white flowers in spring and dark green, needlelike leaves.

❧ Rose campion (*Lychnis coronaria*) has felty, gray foliage and brilliant magenta flowers. It was grown on this continent before the American Revolution.

❧ Bee-balm (*Monarda didyma*) has red flowers that attract hummingbirds, as well as pink, white, and purple cultivars that are handsome in the garden and in arrangements. This native plant was used as a tea substitute during the American Revolution.

❧ Feverfew (*Tanacetum parthenium,* also known as *Chrysanthemum parthenium*), has white, daisylike flowers that last all summer and through light frosts. It was brought to the United States by early settlers.

Best Unusual Perennials

Unusual plants make a welcome addition to any perennial garden. Plant some pheasant's-eye (*Adonis amurensis*), a late-winter woodland gem with bright yellow flowers and fernlike foliage; hardy begonia (*Begonia grandis*), which has pink flowers in early fall and red undercoated leaves; yellow corydalis (*Corydalis lutea*), which has tiny, bright yellow flowers nestled among elegant, blue-green foliage in late spring to fall; small's beard-tongue (*Penstemon smallii*), which has charming pink and white flowers in early summer; and false solomon's-seal (*Smilacina racemosa*), a handsome native plant with graceful, arching foliage and clusters of white flowers in spring.

Foxglove

Bee-balm

Best Foliage Perennials

Perennials with eye-catching foliage include 'Silver Mound' artemisia (*Artemisia schmidtiana* 'Silver Mound'), which has delicate, silvery, needlelike leaves that form neat mounds when grown in full sun; 'Royal Red' heuchera (*Heuchera villosa* 'Royal Red'), a shade-garden gem that has large, maplelike leaves with glossy, dark wine-red coloring; variegated yellow flag (*Iris pseudacorus* 'Variegata'), with tall, swordlike leaves edged in creamy yellow; white Nancy (*Lamium maculatum* 'White Nancy'), with low-growing silver leaves edged in green; and plume poppy (*Macleya cordata*), a perennial giant with huge, deeply lobed green leaves undercoated with grayish, felty texture.

Best Perennials for Shady Places

Perennials that need shade to look their loveliest include lady's-mantle (*Alchemilla vulgaris*), with sprays of tiny chartreuse flowers from spring into summer; goatsbeard (*Aruncus dioicus*), with soaring plumes of white flowers in late spring; pink turtlehead (*Chelone lyonii*), with pink flowers in late summer; black Snakeroot (*Cimicifuga racemosa*), with towering spires of white flowers in summer; Christmas Rose (*Helleborus niger*), with brilliant white flowers in late winter; Virginia bluebells (*Mertensia virginica*), with rich blue flowers in early spring woodlands; and primrose (*Primula* spp.), with sprightly pink, red, white, or yellow flowers in spring.

Best Perennials for Dry Climates

Drought-tolerant perennials include yarrow (*Achillea millefolium*), which has flowers in white, yellow, or pink pastels on feathery, aromatic foliage; butterfly weed (*Asclepias tuberosa*), which has bright orange flowers throughout summer; yellow epimedium (*Epimedium* x *versicolor* 'Sulphureum'), which has yellow flowers in early spring and is excellent for dry shade and poor soil; flowering spurge (*Euphorbia corollata*), which has small white flowers on top of elegantly slim foliage all summer; blanket-flower (*Gaillardia aristata*), which has showy yellow and red flowers throughout summer; and showy sedum (*Sedum spectabile*), which has cool green succulent foliage with bright pink flowers in late summer.

Best Perennials for Wet Places

Perennials that thrive in constantly moist settings, such as bogs or marshes, include marsh marigold (*Caltha palustris*), turtlehead (*Chelone lyonii*), Kamchatka bugbane (*Cimicifuga simplex* 'White Pearl'), mallow (*Hibiscus moscheutos*), bigleaf ligularia (*Ligularia dentata*), cardinal flower (*Lobelia cardinalis*), and Japanese primrose (*Primula japonica*). Some irises also like wet conditions. They include Louisiana irises (hybrids and species of *Iris foliosa, Iris fulva,* and *Iris giganticaerulea*), which have flowers in many colors; 'Dorothea K. Williamson,' a cultivar with wine-red blossoms, is the hardiest; and yellow flag iris (*Iris pseudacorus*), which has bright yellow flowers in late spring, and handsome, arching foliage wands.

Yarrow

Spurge

Color Cues

*U*nsure whether a specific color will fit into your perennial garden? First try an annual flower with a similar hue. If it works, you can replace the annual with a long-lasting perennial.

■ *Plant a mixture of early-, mid-, and late-blooming varieties of a single perennial in the same garden to keep it in colorful flower all season long. Or plant annuals along with perennials.*

■ *Perennial flowers with warm colors, such as reds and oranges, usually prefer the bright rays of hot summer sun.*

Purchasing Plants by Mail

When you order plants by mail, always specify a delivery date. That way, plants will not arrive when you're away. If you're unexpectedly out of town the week delivery is due, call the nursery and ask if it can delay sending the plants.

Bare-root plants often are shipped in wood shavings, peat moss, or other material. Unpack them as soon as they arrive, then add compost to the soil when planting them. Avoid chemical fertilizers because they can be harsh and burn tender bare roots. Dip the roots in a bucket of water before placing the plant in the hole.

DEFENSIVE MANEUVERS

Many invasive plants, such as ribbon grass and lily-of-the-valley, do not have room to spread rampantly when placed in soil pockets bounded by tree roots. Place fast-spreading flowers in soil pockets deep enough to cover their roots, and the plants will thrive in contained clumps rather than overrunning your woodland garden.

- **Set plants at the right level.** Plants should be set in the ground at the same level they grew the previous season. You can see marks of the former depth on the dormant roots. Provide adequate space so that new roots are not crowded. Dig a hole several inches larger in diameter than the width of the roots and spread roots out so they can get established quickly.

- **Reduce soil preparation time.** Dig a deep, properly enriched hole for each plant rather than working the entire garden plot.

- **Deter invasive weeds.** Make sure that all unworked areas are heavily mulched.

- **Water transplants regularly.** Keep the soil evenly moist, but not soggy, for the first week after planting.

MORE WAYS WITH MULCH

- Many communities now give away one of the most effective soil conditioners: composted leaf mulch. This organic matter is an all-purpose additive that lightens clay soils by increasing drainage capability and thickens sandy soils by building up moisture retention. Call your local government to see how you can obtain some.

Use mulch around perennials to . . .

- enrich the soil around your perennials each year.
- smother many annual weed seeds.
- control the number of self-sown seedlings from your favorite perennials. If you find you have too many self-seeders, mulch heavily when the seedlings are still tiny. If you want more plants, don't mulch at all so the seeds can sprout on the bare earth.
- protect new transplants during the winter.

Weeding Out the Competition

Weeds not only crowd out flowers but also deplete soils of essential nutrients. Before planting a new perennial in a garden bed, be sure to clear out all unwanted competitors for space and nourishment.

Use large foliage plants, such as hostas (shown above), to reduce weeds in your garden. The leaves from these plants completely shade the ground beneath them, preventing weed seeds from germinating.

PREVENT POWDERY MILDEW

The summer beauty of perennials, such as garden phlox (shown below) and bee-balm, often is marred by a disfiguring, powdery white mildew. Even if these plants don't appear to be crowded, thin them to allow for good air circulation among the divisions. This will help discourage or even eliminate the disease.

Fall Chores

Fall Cleanup

Fall is a good time to give your garden a physical examination. When raking leaves and cutting back dead stems, check carefully for the presence of weeds or diseased plants and eliminate both promptly. Cleaning up debris eliminates hiding places where pests can overwinter.

Fall Soil Test

Before shutting down your garden for the winter, have your soil tested. Call your local county cooperative extension agent and ask for instructions. A soil test will give you information on the pH (acidity) of your soil, as well as suggestions for any additives needed to improve fertility. Correcting soil deficiencies in the fall will make spring planting easier and smoother.

High-Stakes Success

Staking is important for many tall-growing flowers such as delphinium (shown at right), Canterbury bells, hollyhock, dahlia, and helenium. Place the stakes in the ground while the plants are still young. Staking after the plant is well established can damage the root system. Set four stakes around the base of the plant, slightly inside where you want the plant to spread. Tie heavy cord or wire to the stakes until the entire plant is encircled. For best effect, use inconspicuous stakes and ties for flowering plants.

Propagating Perennials

Self-Seeding

When propagating self-seeding perennials, do as they do—simply scatter the seed on open ground in midsummer. Foxgloves, feverfew, rose mallow, and columbines are among the many perennials that spread their charms by this easy method.

Root Cuttings

Perennials that can be propagated from root cuttings include bear's-breech (*Acanthus mollis*), Italian bugloss (*Anchusa azurea*), butterfly weed (*Asclepias tuberosa*), Siberian bugloss (*Brunnera macrophylla*), Persian cornflower (*Centaurea dealbata*), common bleeding-heart (*Dicentra spectabilis*), gas plant (*Dictamnus albus*), Oriental poppy (*Papaver orientale*), Stokes' aster (*Stokesia laevis*), and mullein (*Verbascum bombyciferum*). When working with root cuttings, plant the end nearest the root crown at the top. If you can't figure out which end is which, place the root horizontally in the growing mixture. Nature will eventually take over and send down roots at the appropriate end, pushing the emerging foliage above the soil.

Tip and Stem Cuttings

Early spring is the best time to propagate from stem cuttings (shown top right) if you don't want to use rooting hormones. It's the time of year when a plant's first flush of vigorous growth has started and the stems are most likely to root and grow, even when cut from the mother plant.

Division

Division, rather than transplanting, is often the best method of moving large, mature perennials, such as peonies (shown bottom right). It is difficult for large, established plants to adjust to transplanting; a small division has a much better chance of successfully settling in.

Chrysanthemums

In the spring, when new plant growth is 3 inches tall, dig up the chrysanthemums (shown at left) and pull them apart. Select sturdy-rooted shoots to transplant to newly prepared fertile soil in a sunny, well-drained location. Space the shoots a foot apart. Cut or pinch off ¾ inch from the top of each newly planted division. When plants are 6 inches tall, prune the plants again to keep them bushy.

Irises

Clumps of bearded iris need to be dug up, divided, and replanted about every three years. Use a sharp knife to separate the rhizomes and make sure each division has a strong section of roots. After separating the rhizomes, trim the foliage to a fan shape. Dig a hole slightly larger than the roots of each division. Set the divisions so that the top half of each rhizome is above ground.

Peonies

It's best to divide peonies (shown at left) every 10 years. In the fall, dig a shallow trench completely around the edge of the clump. Then pry under the root mass with a spade. Use a hose to wash away the soil so you can see where the growing points are. Use a sturdy, sharp knife to make divisions, making sure that no division has fewer than three eyes or growing points. Be sure to keep the roots moist and replant the divisions as soon as possible. To plant a new peony division, dig a deep hole in a sunny location. To encourage sturdy growth, add compost and bonemeal to the planting hole. Set divisions about 3 feet apart, making sure that eyes are 1 to 2 inches below the soil. Mulch the plants for winter. It will take at least two years for three-eye divisions to bloom significantly.

ANNUALS

"Hurray, rain—and the hour arrives for transplanting annuals from the seed frame. All around the place I put them—annual border, of course, perennial border, between newer peonies and newer shrubbery, even between rows in the vegetable garden."

Writings of the Plain Dirt Gardener

Starting Plants from Seed

- Most annuals should be started indoors from seed six to eight weeks before the last predicted spring frost in your area. Begonia, coleus, dianthus, impatiens, lobelia, geranium, pansy, petunia, salvia, and snapdragon (shown above) will take longer.

- Sow small seeds indoors in flats of sterilized mix. Drop seeds into shallow rows without crowding, then cover them lightly. Keep the flats moist and warm, moving them to bright light when the first seedlings pop through the mix.

- After two sets of true leaves form, shift seedlings from flats to individual small pots. Carefully remove a seedling with plenty of roots and soil, then plant it deep enough so it doesn't fall over. Use sanitized pots and soil.

- As soon as the surface of the ground is frost free, you can broadcast seeds of hardy annuals such as bachelor's buttons, larkspurs, shirley poppies, and other frost-resistant annuals.

- You can sow tender annuals directly in the garden in May. Zinnia, marigold, portulaca, celosia, salvia, cosmos, sunflower, dianthus, four-o'clock, nasturtium, morning glory, cornflower, and snapdragon are just some of the quick-growing annuals you can plant for a summer of color.

Planting Pointers

- Before you set out any young transplants in the garden, be sure the planting bed is well prepared. If the soil is packed hard, the seedlings will not prosper.

- Before you put your plants in the ground, remove them from their plastic growing containers. To do this, grasp the base of the plants with one hand and turn the container upside down. Generally, the plants will just slip out; if you have trouble, gently tap the bottom of the container with a trowel. If the plastic is extra thin, it might be easier to just tear the container away from the roots rather than trying to knock the plants out.

- After removing plants from their growing containers, separate them so they can be planted at the proper intervals in the garden. Use a sharp knife and cut around each plant, gently pulling and working the roots free. Keep the soil moist at all times so it won't fall away from the roots.

- To plant seedlings, dig a hole slightly larger than the root ball of the plant (shown top right). After placing the plant in the hole, fill in around it with soil, then water it heavily to eliminate air pockets around the roots.

- Space seedlings at prescribed intervals in the garden. Don't worry if they look sparse; well-tended plants grow quickly and will fill in the bare spots in a few weeks. For instance, dwarf marigolds (shown bottom right), planted at the proper intervals and kept well watered, will completely fill the garden with color in as little as five weeks.

- When transplanting young annual seedlings into the garden during warm weather, it's important to protect them from the drying rays of the sun for a week or so until they become established.

Best Annuals

Best Warm-Weather Annuals

Annuals that thrive in hot weather include flowering maple (*Abutilon* spp.), love-in-a-puff (*Cardiospermum halicacabum*), cup-and-saucer vine (*Cobaea scandens*), California poppy (*Eschscholzia californica*), basket flower (*Gaillardia pulchella*), gazania (*Gazania ringens*), globe amaranth (*Gomphrena globosa*), strawflower (*Helichrysum bracteatum*), New Guinea impatiens (*Impatiens* spp.), moonflower, red summer cypress (*Kochia scoparia* var. *trichophylla*), lantana, tree mallow (*Lavatera trimestris*), tidy-tips (*Layia platyglossa*), southern star (*Oxypetalum caeruleum*), poppies (*Papaver* spp.), balck-eyed Susan (*Rudbeckia hirta* 'Gloriosa Daisy'), verbena, and vinca.

Best Cool-Weather Annuals

Annuals that bloom beautifully in cool weather include the common pansy (*Viola* x *wittrockiana*), a plant that does well as long as the ground doesn't freeze, and snapdragon, calendula, bachelor's button (*Cenaurea cyanus*), most of the annual chrysanthemums, California poppies, blanket-flowers (*Gaillardia pulchella*), annual stocks (*Matthiola incana* 'Annua'), *Phlox drummondii*, most of the salvias, sweet alyssum (*Lobularia maritima*), the verbenas, and the sleepy daisy (*Xanthisma texana*).

Best Annuals for Drying

Many annuals are beautiful when dried. Among the best for drying are hollyhock blossoms, zinnias, and cosmos dried in sand or silica gel; love-lies-bleeding, prince's feather (*Amaranthus hybridus* var. *erythrostachys*), cockscomb, star flower, statice, globe amaranth, love-in-a-mist, and plumed celosia hung upside down and air-dried in a dark, dry spot; and snapdragons dried in silica gel. Bells-of-Ireland should be hung to dry one stalk at a time. Most of the ornamental grasses, including hare's tail grass (*Lagurus ovatus*), quaking grass (*Briza maxima* and *Briza minor*), foxtail millet (*Setaria italica*), and squirreltail grass (*Hordeum jubatum*), dry perfectly when hung by bunches upside down in a dry room, but they must be picked when fresh. The leaves of dusty-miller are also elegant when pressed and dried.

Bachelor's Button

Globe Amaranth

Best Annuals for Dry Places

Annuals that thrive in dry conditions include prickly poppy (*Argemone* spp.), Swan River daisy (*Brachycome iberidifolia*), cosmos (*Cosmos bipinnatus* and *Cosmos sulphureus*), tassel flower (*Emilia javanica*), California poppy (*Eschscholzia californica*), gazania (*Gazania ringens*), globe amaranth (*Gomphrena globosa*), strawflower (*Helichrysum bracteatum*), Mexican tulip poppy (*Hunnemannia fumariifolia*), red summer cypress (*Kochia scoparia* var. *trichophylla*), tree mallow (*Lavatera trimestris*), blazing star (*Mentzelia lindleyi*), opium poppy (*Papaver somniferum*), black-eyed Susan (*Rudbeckia hirta* 'Gloriosa Daisy'), moss rose (*Portulaca grandiflora*), and immortelle (*Xeranthemum annuum*).

Best Annuals for Foliage

Some annual plants with striking foliage are Jacob's-coat (*Acalypha wilkesiana*), garden orach (*Atriplex hortensis*), red Malabar spinach (*Basella alba* 'Rubra'), ornamental kale (*Brassica oleracea*), caladium (*Caladium* x *hortulanum*), dwarf canna (*Canna* x *generalis*), dusty-miller (*Centaurea cineraria* or *Chrysanthemum ptarmiciflorum* 'Silver Feather'), elephant's-ear (*Colocasia esculenta*), bush morning glory (*Convolvulus tricolor*), snow-on-the-mountain (*Euphorbia marginata*), fennel (*Foeniculum vulgare*), red hedging hibiscus (*Hibiscus acetosella* 'Red Shield'), hops (*Humulus japonicus*), bloodleaf (*Iresine herbstii*), curled mallow (*Malva verticillata* var. *crispa*), fountain grass (*Pennisetum setaceum*), Irish lace (*Tagetes filifolia*), dwarf nasturtium (*Tropaeolum minus* 'Alaska Mixed'), and canary creeper (*Tropaeolum peregrinum*).

Best Annuals for Shade

Annuals that can tolerate some shade include bedding begonias (*Begonia* x *semperflorens-cultorum*), browallia, caladium, Madagascar periwinkle (*Catharanthus roseus*), coleus, hops (*Humulus japonicus*), polka-dot plant (*Hypoestes phyllostachya*), impatiens, monkey flower (*Mimulus* x *hybridus*), all the nicotianas, black-eyed Susan vine (*Thunbergia alata*), wishbone flower (*Torenia fournieri*), and pansies.

Best Annuals for Hanging Baskets

Annuals that look great and trail properly for hanging baskets include browallia (*Browallia speciosa*), Madagascar periwinkle (*Catharanthus roseus*), Queen Anne's pocket vine (*Cucumis melo*), Mexican cigar plant (*Cuphea playcentra*), Kenilworth ivy (*Cymbalaria muralis*) lantana (*Lantana* spp.), flowering oregano (*Origanum rotundifolium*), ivy geranium (*Pelargonium peltatum*), nasturtium (*Tropaeolum majus*), black-eyed Susan vine (*Thunbergia alata*), and vinca (*Vinca major* and *Vinca minor*).

Strawflower

Torenia

Color Your World

Get the jump on summer color in the spring with started flats of annual flowers. They'll transform a plain yard almost overnight, and they're available in a wide array of colors and varieties.

■ Use annuals in bright, exciting colors, such as celosia (shown bottom left) to make a garden appear smaller. Use cool tones to make it seem larger. Remember, too, that colors look paler as they recede.

■ To create the illusion of perspective in a garden, choose different cultivars of the same species of plant, with flower color ranging from bright to medium to pale, even white. Start at the front of the border with the darkest color. Set lighter-colored plants behind it, then use even lighter colors. When viewed together, the colors will look as though they are fading into the distance.

■ Colorful annuals can be showstoppers when you mix them according to texture and height, interweaving low plants with tall, spiky ones. Winged everlastings (*Ammobium alatum*), for example, have 3-foot-tall stems topped with small, white, everlasting flowers. Giant cultivars of cannas produce 7-foot columns of upright foliage topped with glorious flame-bright flowers. The brilliant feathered blossoms of the crested types of celosia exhibit sharp-pointed 1-foot plumes on top of 2-foot-tall plants. Tall-growing salvias can reach 4 feet high and come in an array of dazzling colors.

■ For a bright, edible border, plant nasturtiums, which have bright yellow, orange, and red flowers. Nasturtium blooms are edible, have a peppery taste, and add color to a salad as well as to your garden.

■ Enliven dull spots around your yard with groups of containers filled with colorful flowering annuals. For added interest, use several sizes of containers.

Buying Guide to Annuals

- Each spring, most nurseries and garden-supply houses stock a wide selection of annual varieties, including marigolds (shown top right) and zinnias (shown bottom right). To be sure you get what your planting scheme calls for, read the plant label before buying. It will identify the variety name, bloom color, and future height of your seedlings.

- When shopping for annuals, remember that the best buy will not always result in the most beautiful plant.

- Choose annuals that have been watered and are not dried out or shriveled. Also, check to see that shade-lovers have been kept under a sunscreen.

- Pop a plant out of its pot and see how tightly the roots are growing. You want to see healthy roots winding through visible planting medium—not a solid mass of roots. Although tightly rooted plants can be untangled, they are never as successful in the garden as younger plants.

- Choose plants that have a lot of buds, but not flowers. When buying cell packs (six or more plants growing in the same container), make sure that all are straight and healthy.

- Look for healthy, young foliage that is neither burned nor broken. Leaves should be green, not yellow, as yellow leaves show signs of starvation.

- You'll generally find short plants to be a better choice than tall, leggy ones. Short plants have lots of basal shoots to produce bushy, compact plants. Tall plants may be rootbound and grow poorly after planting.

Watering Dos and Don'ts

■ If possible, water annuals in the morning on days with a sunny forecast so foliage will not stay wet too long.

■ When seedlings are hardened off, it's easy to forget how much water they require. Suddenly these tiny plants are out in the open air, where soil and leaf evaporation occur at a much faster rate than when the plants were indoors or in the greenhouse. Make sure the small seedlings get plenty of water, but never use fertilizer at this early stage of growth.

■ If you're adding water to peat-based potting mixes, try these simple tips. For small amounts, put the mix into a plastic bag, add water, and then knead the bag. For larger amounts, use a container like a wheelbarrow, add the mix, then scoop out a center hole and add warm, not cold, water, continually blending. Never add the mix to water; instead, always add water to the mix.

■ Annuals grown in containers need to be watered often because they dry out faster than they do in the ground. Every week or two, while watering, add a soluble fertilizer at half or quarter strength to stimulate growth and constant flowering. To keep growth uniform, rotate the pots weekly.

■ You're not alone in disliking cold showers or cold bathwater. Plants hate cold water, too. This is especially true when they are seedlings or growing in pots where there isn't enough soil to absorb the shock. Always water young plants with cool or tepid water, never icy cold water.

■ Place a small, flat stone on top of soil to deflect the stream of water that comes out of a watering can and to prevent a hole from developing in the soil.

Making a Moss Basket

All you need to make a moss basket is a wire frame, green sphagnum moss, potting soil, and some blooming annuals.

- *Moisten the sphagnum moss before you begin, then use clumps of the moss to line the wire frame. If the moss won't stay in place, tie it with florist's wire.*

- *Poke holes in the sphagnum moss at various spots around the sides of the basket. Tuck a seedling or two into each hole, then fill the basket to the rim with potting soil.*

- *Plant a cluster of annuals in the top of the basket by pulling back some of the soil with your hand. When done, water the plants thoroughly.*

TESTING THE SOIL

- To test soil for planting readiness, squeeze a handful of it. If it stays together, it is too wet for you to work.

- Most warmth-loving annuals will survive in somewhat cooler conditions if their soil is not too cold. If you plan to grow warm-season annuals in the North, use a soil thermometer to find out when the soil is warm enough to set them out.

- Until soil conditions are right for planting, keep seedlings in a protected spot. Water them everyday; there is little medium around their roots, so they can dry out quickly.

Care and Feeding

■ Exercise care when fertilizing annuals. Too much nitrogen generally causes lots of lush foliage growth and little flower development. Use a fertilizer with a higher concentration of phosphorus, which helps flowering.

■ To mix fertilizer, use plastic soft-drink or milk bottles. Following the directions on the fertilizer container, mix a number of small batches of fertilizer and fill several plastic bottles. Then label them with future dates when your plants will again need a boost of plant food.

■ Because most annuals like full sun, you can let more light into a shady garden by removing the lower branches of nearby trees. If the shade is still too dense to allow you many plant choices, have a tree service selectively remove higher branches to lighten the canopy of leaves overhead. Or, select shade-loving annuals such as impatiens and begonias.

■ Many gardeners are looking for a natural way to fight insect pests. For those gardeners, several companies offer the eggs of such insect predators as ladybugs, praying mantises, and green lacewings. After hatching, these beneficial insects will combat many harmful pests.

Just a Pinch

■ To ensure nonstop color until frost, remove blooms from your annuals as soon as they fade. This procedure, called deadheading, ensures maximum and continuous blooming all summer. If you allow blossoms to form seed heads, flower production will stop. You can also promote growth by regularly cutting fresh flowers, such as snapdragon (top right), for indoor bouquets.

■ Many annuals, including sweet alyssum, lobelia (bottom right), petunia, and candytuft, need rejuvenating in midsummer. To encourage fresh growth and more flowers, use pruning shears to cut the stems back by one-third.

Fall Chores

After you've pulled up dead annuals and added them to the compost pile (along with gathered leaves, twigs, and the rest of the horticultural rubbish), give the soil a final rake. Then mulch the open soil, either with an additional layer of shredded leaves or perhaps a bushel or two of pine needles. You'll find the neat and orderly look of the mulch will contribute to the look of the winter garden. Till it in the spring to add organic matter to the soil.

- Avoid placing containers of annuals where heat becomes intense, such as against a west wall or in windy locations.
- Fill containers with sterilized all-purpose potting soil that has a high content of sphagnum peat moss. The peat will help the soil retain moisture, preventing contained plants from drying out quickly on hot summer days.

- Tall, leggy stems are a common malady of such annuals as petunia (shown at right), geranium, browallia, begonia, and impatiens (shown below). Keep them bushy and blooming by pinching back stems just above a set of leaves. This will stimulate new side branching and flower formation within a couple of weeks.

SPECIAL PLANTS

Best Ground Covers

Best Shade-Tolerant Ground Covers

➧ Shrubby ground covers for shady areas include the elegant evergreen spreading English yew (*Taxus bacata* 'Repandens'), the evergreen blackberry relative *Rubus calycinoides,* and deciduous bunchberry (*Cornus canadensis*).

➧ For flowering ground covers in light shade and moist soil, plant a spreading perennial, such as dwarf Chinese astilbe (*Astilbe chinensis* 'Pumila'), which has fluffy pink flowers, or lungworts (*Pulmonaria* spp.), which sport beautifully speckled foliage and flowers in blue, violet, red, or white.

➧ Lilyturf (*Liriope* or *Ophiopogon* spp.) gives a clumping grasslike effect, while Irish moss (*Arenaria* spp.), Scotch moss (*Sagina* spp.), and many native mosses form soft green carpets in shade.

Best Drought-Tolerant Ground Covers

Some of the prettiest water-thrifty ground covers are herbs. Groups of these species make charming ground-cover combinations for full sun.

➧ Woolly yarrow (*Achillea tomentosa*) forms a flat, dense mat of furry leaves, topped in summer with clusters of yellow flowers. Mat-forming thymes look great planted near lamb's-ears (*Stachys byzantina*) or catmint (*Nepta* x *faassenii*).

➧ Creeping rosemary (*Rosmarinus officinalis* 'Prostratus') drapes beautifully over banks or walls and features blue flowers. Small, evergreen shrubby santolinas (*Santolina chamae-cyparissus* and *Santolina virens*) are effective intermingled in drifts.

Best Fast-Spreading Ground Covers

➧ Ground covers that fill in quickly include African daisy, ajuga, bearberry, bellflower, carmel creeper, crown vetch, Algerian ivy, lamium, mondo grass, moneywort, sedum, snow-in-summer, verbena, and yellowroot.

Best Ground Covers to Withstand Traffic

➧ Chamomile (*Chamaemelum nobile*) forms a low, dense mat of finely divided evergreen leaves with small yellow or white flowers. Mow it after flowering. 'Treneague,' a nonflowering cultivar, stays low without mowing.

➧ Frogfruit (*Phyla nodiflora*) is well adapted to heat. It survives with little water but looks better with regular irrigation. The creeping stems have small, oval, gray-green leaves and lavender flowers that attract bees.

➧ Irish moss (*Arenaria verna*) and Scotch moss (*Sagina subulata*) cover small areas with a soft, velvetlike carpet. In cool climates, plant them in sunny locations in rich, moist soil. Give them afternoon shade in warmer areas.

Chamomile

Best Ground Covers with Showy Flowers

➤ Plants that make grand ground covers and have beautiful blossoms include African daisy, agapanthus, ajuga, astilbe, bellflower, bougainvillea, candytuft, carmel creeper, cinquefoil, crown vetch, daylily, deutzia, forget-me-not, gazania, geranium, heath, heather, hosta, trailing lantana, lily-of-the-valley, creeping phlox, moss or maiden pink, potentilla, St. John's wort, snow-in-summer, speedwell, spirea, and verbena.

Best Ground Covers with Variegated Foliage

➤ Hostas offer some of the most dramatic variegated leaves, blending wonderfully with smaller ground covers, such as periwinkle.
➤ Spotted dead nettle (*Lamium maculatum*) has silver-and-green leaves that look wonderful under flowering shrubs.
➤ The cultivar 'Beacon Silver' has pink flowers; another, 'White Nancy,' has white flowers.
➤ Lilyturf (*Liriope muscari*), a ground cover frequently used in the shade of trees and shrubs and along walks in the humid Southeast, is available in several handsome variegated forms, including 'Silvery Sunproof' and 'Variegata.'

Lamium

Best Ground Covers for Fall and Winter Interest

➤ Cotoneasters feature bright red berries that often last into winter. In fall, the foliage of the deciduous species turns red.
➤ Some varieties of wintercreeper (*Euonymus fortunei*) offer exceptional fall interest. The leaves of 'Colorata' turn a deep purple in fall. 'Gracilis' has attractive leaves variegated with white or cream, some of which become pink in cold weather. Creeping mahonia (*Mahonia repens*) has purple leaflets in winter; dark blue berries may remain through winter.

PLANTING GROUND COVERS

■ Save time and effort on lawn maintenance by reducing the size of your lawn and devoting more yard space to ground covers, such as ajuga (below). They don't require mowing, and they have low-moisture needs. Also, ground covers often grow better than grass under trees and shrubs.

■ To save money, buy ground covers in flats of 100 plants. (Individually potted ground cover plants cost much more.) One flat covers about 30 square feet.

■ Mulch with organic matter right after you plant a ground cover. The mulch will save you hours of weeding and watering by smothering weeds and conserving soil moisture.

Best Herbs

Best Herbs for Flower Gardens

❥ Herbs that make beautiful additions to flower gardens include anise, bee-balm, borage, calendula, catmint, chamomile, chervil, chives, clary sage, coneflower, coriander, costmary, cumin, fennel, feverfew, foxglove, hyssop, lavender, rosemary, scented geraniums, sweet woodruff, tansy, thyme, violets, and yarrow.

Best Herbs for Containers

❥ Herbs that adapt well to containers include basil, bay, borage, catmint, catnip, chervil, chives, Greek oregano, hyssop, lavender, lemon balm, marjoram, mint, parsley, rosemary, sage, savory, scented geraniums, sorrel, tarragon, and thyme.

Best Herbs with Variegated Leaves

❥ Orange mint (*Mentha* x *piperita* var. *citrata*) has dark green leaves edged with purple, and pineapple mint (*Mentha suaveolens* 'Variegata') has green leaves with white patches.

❥ Golden sage (*Salvia officinalis* 'Aurea') has green leaves edged with yellow, purple sage (*Salvia officinalis* 'Purpurea') has green leaves edged in purplish red, and tricolor sage (*Salvia officinalis* 'Tricolor') has cream, purplish-red, and pink leaves.

❥ Lemon thyme (*Thymus* x *citriodorus* 'Aureus') has green and yellow leaves, silver lemon thyme (*Thymus citriodorus* 'Argenteus') has leaves variegated with green and silver, silver thyme (*Thymus vulgaris* 'Argenteus') has silver and green leaves, and golden thyme (*Thymus vulgaris* 'Aureus') has yellow and green leaves.

Best Herbs for Shade

❥ Herbs that can tolerate and even thrive in varying degrees of shade include angelica, chervil, chives, coltsfoot, costmary, foxglove, lady's-mantle, lemon balm, lovage, mint, parsley, sweet cicely, sweet flag, sweet woodruff, and tarragon.

Best Herbs for Moist Conditions

❥ Herbs that prefer or can tolerate wet conditions include angelica, comfrey, foxglove, horsetail, lady's-mantle, lovage, marsh mallow, mint, pennyroyal, sorel, sweet flag, sweet woodruff, valerian, and violets.

Best Drought-Tolerant Herbs

❥ Herbs that prefer dry conditions include borage, chives, fennel, feverfew, germander, lavender, Roman chamomile, rosemary, sage, savory, southernwood, thyme, wormwood, and yarrow.

Best Herbs for Freezing

❥ Herbs that keep their flavor when frozen include basil, borage, chives, dill, lemongrass, mint, oregano, sage, savory, sorrel, sweet woodruff, tarragon, and thyme. Simply clean and dry the leaves, then put them in sealed plastic bags (removing all air before sealing) or another airtight container for freezing.

Borage

Dill

Tall Herbs

❧ Herbs that work best when grown toward the back of a garden or planted as background include angelica (to 8 feet), bay (40-foot tree, kept much shorter with pruning), bee-balm (to 3 feet), dill (to 3 feet), fennel (3 to 4 feet), lemongrass (3 to 4 feet), lovage (4 to 6 feet), mugwort (4 to 6 feet), mullein (to 6 feet), sage (1 to 3 feet, depending on variety), southernwood (3 to 5 feet), sweet cicely (to 3 feet), tansy (to 4 feet), and yarrow (to 5 feet).

Small Herbs

❧ Herbs that work best in the front of a garden or in pots or window boxes include miniature basil, boxwood, catnip, chamomile, chives, germander, hyssop, juniper, lavender, lavender cotton, parsley, rosemary, sage, southernwood, sweet woodruff, thyme, violets, winter savory, and wormwood.

Best Herbs for Topiaries

❧ Herbs suitable for training into standards, spirals, and multiple levels include bay, curry plant, juniper, lavender, lavender cotton, lemon verbena, licorice plant, rosemary, sage, scented geraniums, and thyme.

Lavender

Indoor/Outdoor Herbs

- Where winters are cold, grow bay, lemongrass, lemon verbena, rosemary, and scented geraniums in pots and bring them indoors during the winter.
- Although they may not last the winter, try planting basil, chervil, chives, coriander, dill, marjoram, oregano, parsley, and thyme in pots and bringing them indoors to a sunny windowsill before frost to continue the harvest of fresh leaves for another month or so.
- Rather than potting tender perennial herbs, such as rosemary or bay, each fall to bring indoors for winter, grow them in pots year-round. Keep the pots outside during the warm season, then move them to a sheltered place, such as a porch, for a few weeks before bringing them inside. If you want them to look as if they were actually planted in the garden, bury the pots up to the rim. Burying will also help them stay moist so you won't need to water as often.

HOMEMADE POTPOURRI

Here's a basic potpourri recipe that can be varied to include your favorite plants and fragrances.

Mix 3 tablespoons of powdered orrisroot with 1 teaspoon of essential oil, such as rose oil. Blend and store, covered, for a few days, shaking occasionally. This allows the orrisroot to absorb the moisture of the oil.

Mix in 1 quart of dried flowers and herbs. Add 2 to 3 tablespoons of spices. Mix well and store, covered, in a container for four to six weeks, stirring occasionally. Pack the potpourri in jars or baskets to keep, to give as gifts, or to crush and use in sachets.

Best Ways with Bulbs

Begonias and Caladiums

❧ Start tuberous begonias and caladiums indoors eight weeks before the last expected frost. Place the tubers in shallow flats filled with moist sphagnum moss and potting soil. Plant the tubers just under the surface of the soil; place caladiums round-side up and tuberous begonias round-side down. Transplant tubers to peat pots after sprouting, and move the young plants outdoors after frost danger.

Dahlias

❧ Start dahlias outdoors after the danger of frost has passed. Plant large tubers 4 inches deep and small ones 2 inches deep. As the plants develop, pinch them back to encourage branching. Dig up the tubers in the fall, wash off the soil, and store them in several inches of moist vermiculite.

❧ Start standard and dwarf varieties of dahlias in the garden in May. Plant tubers 4 inches deep in well-worked soil; plant small tubers only 2 inches deep. As the plants develop, pinch them back to encourage branching. Tall varieties of dahlias need to be staked, so be sure to insert a stout stake into the ground nearby at planting time.

❧ If you plan to start dahlias from seeds, be sure the planting bed is in a loose, friable condition. Sprinkle seeds over the soil's surface and cover them with about ½ inch of soil. Water, and in a week or so, dahlias should be sprouting.

Gladiolus

❧ Plant gladiolus corms about 3 inches deep in clusters of four, eight, or more. Plant only after all danger of frost has passed. Space individual corms about 6 inches apart. For continuous color, plant new corms every two weeks.

❧ In the fall, leave the plants in the ground until the foliage yellows. Then dig the corms, cut off the tops, and cure them in a warm room for several weeks. When cured, the corms should be stored in net bags in a cool, dark, dry location.

Cannas

❧ Start canna lilies indoors a month before the last frost in the spring or directly outdoors after frost danger has passed.

Cannas like a rich, moist soil and should be planted horizontally 1 inch below the soil's surface.

Lily-of-the-Valley

❧ You can have an early spring indoors with forced lily-of-the-valley pips or roots. Pot them in soil, sand, or peat moss so that the top edge of each pip barely protrudes above the soil. Keep the pips well watered at all times, and set them in a warm location. In a few weeks, the plants will bloom.

Spider Lilies

❧ Lycoris, often called spider lily, is best planted in April for blooms in August or September. Foliage doesn't appear until after the flowers are spent, and the plant will remain green all winter long in southern regions. The lilies will thrive in any fertile soil. Set them 2 inches deep in a sunny or partially shady location. To ensure good blooms, mix in a generous amount of bonemeal at planting time.

Narcissus

❧ Paperwhite narcissus are one of several bulbs you can force into bloom immediately after you purchase them.

Dahlias

Bury them in small stones or soil, add water until it reaches the bases of the bulbs, and place the pot in a bright area. Keep the bulbs well watered and you'll enjoy their fragrant blooms in six weeks or less. The most common white-flowering variety is 'Paperwhite Grandiflora.' A yellow-flowering variety, 'Grand Soleil d'Or,' also is available. For a continuous show of color, start new pots of paperwhites every two weeks. Throw them away after they bloom.

Tips for the Tender

Tender bulbs cannot be left in the ground over winter like hardy bulbs. Instead, they must be dug up at the end of each season and stored until spring.

- Color—that's what you'll get when you plant tender bulbs. Few other plant groups can boast the variety of colors and combinations of colors found in this family of bulbs. The most popular tender bulbs include gladiolus, canna lily, dahlia, tuberous begonia, and caladium.
- During the winter, check the condition of your stored dahlias, gladiolus, caladiums, canna lilies, and other tender bulbs. If the bulbs look shriveled or dry, add sufficient moisture to the storage medium. If the bulbs look as if they are starting to decay, they are probably too wet and should be removed and stored under drier conditions. Throw away rotting bulbs.

HINTS FOR THE HARDY

Often the first plants to bloom in the spring, hardy bulbs are a gardener's delight after a dreary winter. Hardy bulbs can be left in the ground indefinitely with only minimum attention.

- The most commonly planted hardy bulbs include tulips, hyacinths, crocus, narcissus, muscari, and alliums (shown below).
- All spring-flowering hardy bulbs must be planted in the fall. Most are not touchy about soil, but they all need good drainage, so avoid low spots.
- Except for standard tulips and hyacinths, all spring-flowering hardy bulbs may be naturalized—grown in grass on hillsides or under trees and allowed to multiply naturally each year. Don't move these plantings until the bulb foliage yellows, however. This allows the bulb to build up strength for bloom the following spring. Narcissus and crocus are especially well-suited for naturalization.
- For visual impact, plant hardy bulbs in groups or clusters of at least a dozen plants. It's also a good idea to use all of one variety and color in a grouping rather than planting a mixture, or your garden will look disorganized.

Best Vines

Plant vines if you want to hide unsightly eaves, camouflage a bare wall, or frame a doorway with color. They are quick growing, easy to maintain, and hardy in even the coldest climates.

Best Vines for Fragrance

➤ Vines that offer fragrant flowers or foliage include sweet autumn clematis, honeysuckle, jasmine, kiwi, madeira vine, moonflower, and rose.

Best Vines for Fruiting

➤ Vines that produce attractive fruit include white and scarlet runner beans, bitter melon, bittersweet, most species of clematis, Virginia creeper, running euonymus, grape, hop vine, kiwi, magnolia vine, rose, scarlet kadsura, and winter creeper.

Best Vines for City Conditions

➤ For city gardens, choose vines that are better able to tolerate pollution, poor soil, and reduced light and air circulation, such as scarlet runner beans, cathedral bells, cypress vine, hop vine, Boston ivy, English ivy, silver-lace vine, and wisteria.

Best Vines for Fall and Winter Interest

➤ For fall flowers, plant sweet autumn clematis (*Clematis paniculata*), golden clematis (*Clematis tangutica*), and silver-lace vine (*Polygonum aubertii*).
➤ Both Boston ivy (*Parthenocissus tricuspidata*) and Virginia creeper (*Parthenocissus quinquefolia*) are noted for their glorious fall color.

➤ Crimson glory vine (*Vitis coignetiae*) has large rounded leaves that turn a brilliant scarlet in fall.
➤ For colorful fruit, plant porcelain berry (*Ampelopsis brevipedunculata*), with its turquoise to deep purple fruits, or American bittersweet (*Celastrus scandens*).

Best Vines for Trellises

➤ Consider *Clematis* x *jackmanii,* a fairly vigorous vine with large purple-blue flowers. There are cultivars with blue, red, or violet blossoms, too.
➤ The evergreen leaves of Carolina yellow jessamine (*Gelsemium sempervirens*) form a delicate green curtain on a trellis, highlighted by fragrant yellow flowers in late winter to early spring.
➤ Potato vine (*Solanum jasminoides*), evergreen in the mildest winters, blooms almost year-round with a froth of bluish-white flowers.
➤ Downy clematis (*Clematis macropetala*) is somewhat smaller than most other clematis, growing 6 to 10 feet; its lavender to powder blue flowers appear in early spring. Scarlet clematis (*Clematis texensis*) is also smaller, growing to about 10 feet. It is more tolerant of dry soil than other clematis.

Wisteria

Clematis

Old Wood...

Prune climbing vines that flower on wood that grew the previous summer soon after blooming. Such plants include vines in the genus *Actinidia,* such as hardy kiwi (*Actinidia arguta*) and *Actinidia kolomikta,* golden-trumpet vine (*Allamanda cathartica*), bougainvillea, Carolina yellow jessamine (*Gelsemium sempervirens*), climbing hydrangea (*Hydrangea anomala* sub. *petiolaris*), jasmine (*Jasminum* spp.), the tender bower vine (*Pandorea jasminoides*), Japanese hydrangea vine (*Schizophragma hydrangeoides*), and wisteria.

...New Wood

Prune climbing vines that flower on new or the current season's growth in late winter. Such vines include trumpet creeper (*Campsis radicans*), honeysuckles (*Lonicera* spp.), mandevilla species, blue passionflower (*Passiflora caerulea*), maypop (*Passiflora incarnata*), silver-lace vine (*Polygonum aubertii*), potato vine (*Solanum jasmininoides*), blue potato vine (*Solanum crispum*), Madagascar jasmine (*Stephanotis floribunda*), and grapes (*Vitis* spp.).

TRAINING VINES AS GROUND COVERS

Many ground-covering vines spread out naturally, but others need training to spread evenly. Use 6-inch wire staples or rocks to direct growth, especially to encourage vines to grow uphill to cover a slope. It also helps to cut back extra-long stems to force side-branching for a thicker, more even cover.

Getting a Grip

Learning how different vines climb will help you decide which kind of support each needs.

- Vines such as grapes (*Vitis* spp.), clematis, and passionflower (*Passiflora* spp.) climb by twisting tendrils or leaf stems around a slender support, such as a wire. Clinging tendrils lend strong support to grapes and more delicate help to clematis and passionflower.
- Vines such as honeysuckle (*Lonicera* spp.), morning glory (*Ipomoea tricolor,* shown at right), and wisteria hoist themselves aloft by twining their stems around wires, stakes, and trellises.
- Vines such as English ivy (*Hedera helix*), climbing fig (*Ficus pumile*), and climbing hydrangea (*Hydrangea anomala* sub. *Petiolaris*) climb by means of aerial roots or holdfasts. The rootlike holdfasts reach into dry crevices, allowing the vines to attach themselves directly to solid walls, fences, and tree trunks. They grow longer to hold securely as the vine's weight increases.
- Some plants grown as vines, including climbing roses (*Rosa* hybrids) and bougainvillea (*Bougainvillea* x *buttiana*), have arching stems that need to be tied to a support to encourage them to grow upward, or they will sprawl on the ground.

Best Ornamental Grasses

Grasses for Different Soils

✦ All the cultivars of fountain grass (*Pennisetum alopecuroides*), blue grama (*Bouteloua gracilis*), sweet vernal grass (*Anthoxanthum odoratum*), silky-spike melic grass (*Melica ciliata*), and purple moor grass grow in acid soils.

✦ Big bluestem (*Andropogon gerardii*) and sideoats grama (*Boutelous curtipendula*) are perfect for alkaline conditions.

✦ Grasses that do well in sandy, dry soils include tufted hair grass (*Deschampsia caespitosa*), weeping love grass (*Eragrostis curvula*), and giant feather grass (*Stipa gigantea*).

✦ For poor soil, choose blue grama, ribbon grass (*Phalaris arundinacea* var. *picta*), or members of the genus *Festuca*.

✦ Feather reed grass (*Calamagrostis acutiflora* var. *stricta*) and tufted hair grass (*Deschampsia caespitosa*) are ideal for heavy clay soils.

Best Grasses for Shade

✦ Grasses for shade include variegated maiden grass, bulbous oat grass, *Festuca gigantea, Glyceria maxima* 'Variegata,' wild oats (*Chasmanthium latifolium*), tufted hair grass (*Deschampsia caespitosa*), bottlebrush grass, *Hakonechoa macra* 'Aureola,' and ribbon grass (*Phalaris arundinacea* var. *picta*).

✦ Most shade-loving plants are sedges—members of the genus *Carex.* They include *Carex buchananii, Carex comans, Carex stricta* 'Bowles's Golden,' *Carex pendula,* and all forms of *Carex morrowii.* Another good shade plant is Fraser sedge (*Cymophyllus fraseri*).

✦ Best annual grasses for shade include cloud grass (*Agrostis nebulosa*) and hare's-tail grass (*Lagurus ovatus).*

Best Drought-Tolerant Grasses

✦ Drought-tolerant grasses include blue grama *(Bouteloua gracilis)*, wood grass (*Sorghastrum avenaceum*), wild oats (*Chasmanthium latifolium*), big bluestem (*Andropogon gerardii*), and switch-grass (*Panicum virgatum*).

✦ Don't overlook most of the *Miscanthus* species and cultivars; they won't tolerate a complete lack of water, but they'll survive with reduced rations.

✦ Another ideal grass in dry conditions is prairie cordgrass (*Spartina pectinata* 'Aureo-marginata'), a real surprise because this grass also does well in wet soils and even water.

Best Small Grasses for Containers

✦ The following will do well if the soil is kept moist and plants are protected from hot sun: sedges, including all of the *Carex* species (except *Carex pendula,* which is too large); *Cyperus* species; smaller members of the genus *Juncus*; and even the smaller horsetails (*Equisetum* spp.).

✦ Many fescues (*Festuca* spp.), especially the various cultivars of *Festuca cinerea* and *Festuca amethystina,* look great in tiny pots. A cultivar of *Festuca scoparia* called 'Pic Carlit' is only 3 inches high and could easily win the garden cuteness award.

Best Variegated Grasses

✦ If you live in a northern climate where zebra grass (*Miscanthus sinensis* 'Zebrinus') won't survive, plant the closely related porcupine grass (*Miscanthus sinensis* 'Strictus'). One of the newer variegated plants available at nurseries, porcupine grass is hardier than zebra grass (it survives in zone 4), and its form is different. Zebra grass has gracefully arching leaves; porcupine grass has ½-inch-wide banded blades. The grasses reach 6 feet tall and are especially beautiful in a waterside setting.

Ribbon Grass

Best Grasses for Prairie Gardens

Plant tall prairie grasses if your garden receives more than 30 inches of rainfall a year; short types do best in drier areas.

❧ Big bluestem (*Andropogon gerardii*) grows 4 to 10 feet tall, and little bluestem (*Schizachyrium scoparium*) reaches a height of 2 to 5 feet.

❧ Blue grama (*Bouteloua gracilis*), native to the High Plains, grows in a bunch about 1½ feet tall when in flower.

❧ Sweetgrass, or basket grass (*Hierochloe odorata*), about 3 feet tall, smells of vanilla and has long been used in making baskets.

❧ Switch-grass (*Panicum virgatum*), 4 to 10 feet tall, has seed heads and blades that turn orange-yellow in winter.

❧ Indian grass (*Sorghastrum avenaceum*, shown below), 2 to 5 feet tall, forms plumelike seed heads in September.

❧ Prairie cordgrass (*Spartina pectinata*) produces 2½-foot blades that wave and fold like fanciful ribbons.

Indian Grass

Grasses for Every Reason

■ To create living sculptures, plant horsetails (*Equisetem* spp.) in small gardens, in simple containers as short-term houseplants, in a water garden, in a troublesome wet spot as accent plants, or in mass in front of a plain or textured wall. These evergreen perennial grasses are truly sculptural, and if properly displayed, they look as though they were created by an artist instead of nature.

■ When choosing ornamental grasses for your landscape, include a few plants for the cutting garden. The beautifully textured flowers of grasses are excellent when cut for fresh bouquets and when dried.

■ If you are tired of cutting all that lawn, clear a large circle or oval of garden toward the center of the yard and plant it with a collection of ornamental grasses, such as maiden grass, shown below. The high point of this island bed could be a mature Ravenna grass plant (*Erianthus ravennae),* a few large eulalia grasses, or one of the new pampas grass cultivars in warmer parts of the country. Surround that planting with a ring of fountain grasses and finish off the edges with a line of dwarf fescues. All you'll need to maintain the grasses are sharpened shears to cut back last year's growth in late February or early March.

VEGETABLES AND FRUITS

"I like to make successive plantings of our favorite vegetables so a fresh supply keeps coming on."

Writings of The Plain Dirt Gardener

Vegetable Gardening Basics

Planting Timetable

Find the average date of the last spring frost in your area, then count forward 10 to 12 weeks to plant onions and leeks; 8 to 10 weeks for peppers; 6 to 8 weeks for tomatoes, cole crops, and head lettuce; and 3 to 4 weeks for okra, squash, cucumbers, and melons.

Get a Jump on Germination

Get a head start by presprouting seeds of peas, beans, or corn. Fold the seeds in a damp paper towel, wrap them in a plastic bag, and put them in a warm, dark place indoors. Check them daily, and as soon as the seeds sprout, sow them in the garden.

WINTER PROPAGATION

January is the perfect time to start vegetable transplants indoors. Sow seeds of eggplants, tomatoes, peppers, cabbages, cauliflower, and broccoli in peat pellets or in low flats. Keep the seedlings well watered and be sure they get at least eight to 10 hours of artificial light a day.

Keep Off the Soil

Be careful where you step. Don't put your weight on the soil you've loosened for plants. Keep to designated pathways, where regular foot traffic will gradually compact the soil into a hard surface that dries quickly and resists weeds.

Moving On

It's easiest to remove transplants from their individual pots if the soil is slightly dry, helping the root ball hold together. Be sure to water all plants thoroughly as soon as you put them in the ground.

Shady Proposition

By planning ahead, you can use one crop to protect another from the glare of the hot summer sun. Let tall plants shade shorter ones. Try putting a row of lettuce or spinach along the north side of a block of asparagus or corn (right), or sowing a patch of salad greens under a clump of sunflowers or a tepee of pole beans.

Sow Easy

Small seeds like those of radishes or carrots tend to clump together, and it's hard to spread them evenly in a row. To make sowing easier, fold the seed packet lengthwise to make a sharp crease that runs to the center of the flap, and align the seeds in the crease. Then tap the packet to drop one seed at a time.

Packing a Punch

Small vegetable plants can make a colorful impact in tight spaces. Compact and prolific, ornamental peppers and patio tomatoes will contribute a fiery red accent to a tiny corner of the garden.

WISE WATERING

Dry soil is especially stressful for tiny plants whose roots are still close to the surface. Be especially careful to water regularly (once a day if needed) after sowing seeds, when seedlings are still small or after setting out transplants in the garden. Fruiting crops also need water when they are flowering and setting their crop. Root vegetables need water as their roots are enlarging.

DIRECT-SEED VEGETABLES

Vegetables that form taproots are stunted by transplanting. They grow best when seeded right in the garden where they are to grow. It's better to directly sow corn, all kinds of beans and peas, certain greens such as Swiss chard or spinach, and root crops such as radishes, carrots, beets, turnips, and parsnips. If your growing season is so short that you must start some of these vegetables indoors, plant them in individual peat pots to minimize root disturbance when you plant them out in the garden.

Best Vegetables

Best Decorative Vegetables

Some of the prettiest vegetables have bright-colored leaves, flowers, or fruits. Plants like ruby chard; pink or lilac ornamental kale; striped eggplants; or red, gold, orange, purple, or chocolate brown peppers make cheerful accents that break the monotony of plain green foliage.

Best Shade-Tolerant Vegetables

If your garden gets less than six hours of sun a day, plant leafy vegetables such as lettuce, spinach, Swiss chard, endive, cabbage, escarole, cress, sorrel, and arugula. In shade, carrots and beets will grow bigger tops than normal, but their roots will be smaller than normal. If there's space for the vines to stretch and sprawl, try pumpkins or winter squash.

Best Drought-Tolerant Vegetables

Once they're past the seedling stage, some vegetables can tolerate a spell of hot, dry weather because they have deep roots. These include asparagus, lima beans, tepary beans, pumpkins and winter squash, okra, Southern peas, chili peppers, peanuts, sweet potatoes, tomatoes, and watermelons. All do best if they are planted in soil that has been loosened to a depth of 1 foot or more and amended with plenty of organic matter.

Best Frost-Tolerant Vegetables

Plant seeds of peas, spinach, lettuce, beets, carrots, and radishes as soon as you can work the ground in spring. These vegetables prefer cool weather and tolerate cold soil and frosty nights. Some cole crops, such as cabbage and cauliflower, can take light frosts but may be stunted by temperatures of 27° to 28° F and below. Other cabbage family crops, such as kale, collards, and Chinese cabbage, can withstand the lower temperatures without any problems.

Best Vegetable Varieties for Short-Season Gardens

In northern and high-mountain gardens, try planting early varieties, such as Royal Burgundy snap bean, Red Ace beet, Emerald Acre cabbage, Earlivee sweet corn, Black-seeded Simpson or Red Sails lettuce, Ace bell peppers, and Sweet 100 cherry tomatoes.

Tomatoes

Radishes

FLAVORFUL FALL VEGETABLES

Some vegetables develop their best flavor and quality during the short days and cool nights of fall.

- Kale, collards, and cabbage become milder and lose any bitterness after a few weeks of cool fall weather.

- Lettuce, spinach, and other greens become very crisp and succulent.

- Kale, cauliflower (shown below), Brussels sprouts, and other cole crops taste sweeter after they've been touched by frost.

- Beets and celeriac develop a surprising sweetness.

- Leeks grow thick and tender and taste sweeter.

- Carrots become incredibly sweet and juicy.

Proper Nutrition

Give plants a boost through these nutritional supplements.

- Vegetables can absorb nutrients through their leaves, as well as through their roots. Spraying or sprinkling a dilute fertilizer solution on the foliage, called foliar feeding, is a good way to boost new transplants or young seedlings that don't have big root systems yet.

- An effective soil enrichment technique is to plant grasses, called "green manure," as a cover crop during the winter months. Till your cleared garden beds after fall harvest, then thickly broadcast, or scatter, grass seeds. Turn the young green shoots under in early spring, or cut them back to the ground a month or so before planting your garden. The shoots will quickly break down and enrich your soil. Popular cover crops include annual rye, hairy vetch, winter barley, buckwheat, clover, and alfalfa. Call your county cooperative extension agent to see which grass is best for your area.

STRAW VS. HAY

Straw, the dried stems and leaves of harvested grains, is preferable to hay as a mulch because it's usually weed free. Second-cutting hay is more expensive but has fewer weed seeds than first-cutting hay. When in doubt, hot-compost the hay before spreading it on the garden.

Vegetable Garden Style

VERTICAL GARDENING

You can save precious ground space by training vining crops—such as climbing peas, pole beans, melons, pumpkins, tomatoes, and squash—on vertical supports.

• A section of chain-link or woven-wire fence can support a big crop. Melons and squash fruits will need sling supports to keep the weight from pulling vines off the fence.

• Other good supports include trellises made of lath stakes or bamboo poles, grow-netting stapled between two upright poles, and sturdy cages made of concrete-reinforcing wire.

Wide-Row Gardening

Wide-row gardening works on the principle that plants sown close together in broad bands produce up to four times as much harvest as the same area planted single file in separate rows. Individual plants may not produce as much as when they're spaced according to seed package instructions, but on the whole, the volume of production will be much greater. There are other benefits, too: Wide-row gardening eliminates a lot of weeding because vegetables grow thickly and choke out weeds. Plants also shade the soil, keeping it moist during hot, dry spells.

Double-Cropping

If you have room only for a small garden, economize the space by doubling-up plantings. You'll get twice the harvest per square foot. To prevent crowding, combine plants with different maturity rates.

• Sow radishes with slower germinating carrots. The radishes will sprout quickly and prevent weed growth. When the radishes are ready to harvest, the carrots can take over.

• Set onions to be used as scallions among cabbage, cauliflower, or Brussels sprouts plants.

• Beets and broccoli also are a good combination. Beets grow rapidly in spring, while broccoli is slower to get established.

Succession Planting and Crop Rotation

Plant legumes, such as beans and peas, to enrich your soil. The roots of these vegetables are host to soil bacteria that extract nitrogen from the air. Thus, in addition to providing a harvest for your table, the legumes also store nitrogen in the soil for other crops.

SECOND CROPPING

Early season vegetables, such as lettuce, peas, carrots, and beets, leave voids in the garden after they are harvested in midsummer. To keep the garden in constant production, reseed empty areas with a quick-growing crop, such as beans. Later in the summer, you can plant more seeds of the cool-season crops for fall harvest.

CONTAINER VEGETABLES

With proper care, most vegetables will grow in containers, but the following typically produce a better harvest: bush and pole beans, beets, carrots, Swiss chard, cucumbers, eggplants, kale, kohlrabi, lettuce, green onions, peas, peppers, potatoes, radishes, turnips, spinach, squash, sweet potatoes, and tomatoes.

Hillside Harvest

Hills are ideal for vining plants that like warm, well-drained soils. These include cucumbers, squash, pumpkins, melons, and gourds. Space the hills about 6 feet apart. Sow several seeds per hill, then thin them to the strongest two or three seedlings. In cool-climate regions, preheat the soil by covering the hill with black plastic for a week before planting. Start seedlings indoors, and set out two or three transplants per hill.

To plant climbing forms of snap, lima, or runner beans in hills, loosen the soil several inches deep in a circle 3 feet wide. Hoe the soil into a raised ring around the edge of the circle. Plant seeds 3 inches apart, then thin the seedlings to stand 6 inches apart. Make a tepee of three or more poles to support the climbing vines.

Container Soil Mix

To make a good all-purpose soil mix for container vegetables, blend equal parts of potting soil or garden soil, finely crumbled compost or leaf mold, and vermiculite, peat moss, or perlite.

Slings and Stakes

- Avoid "fallout" from heavy, vertically grown crops by making support slings to cradle them until they ripen on the vine. Cut old sheets, nylons, or towels into squares, then knot the corners and use them to tie up pumpkins, cucumbers, and squash.
- Climbing vines get heavy and need a sturdy support. If you use any kind of twine, make sure it's thick and strong. Use natural fiber, not synthetic twine, so you can toss the whole tangle of vines and twine onto the compost pile.
- It's hard to secure a plant to a smooth, slippery, metal or wood pole. With nothing for the ties to catch onto, they slide down the pole. For better support, use rough-cut lumber, saplings with bark and limb stubs, or bamboo.

Pick of the Crop

Follow these hints to produce the best results with favorite vegetables and fruits.

Asparagus

- Once asparagus gets going, it requires less care than nearly any other garden crop. Plant it in April, using disease-resistant varieties.
- Asparagus roots are available through garden centers and catalogs. You can buy either 2-year-old or 1-year-old stock. The 2-year-old stock will give you a harvestable crop sooner.
- Asparagus does well in many kinds of soil, from sandy to heavy, but it does enjoy good drainage. For your asparagus plot, prepare soil at least 12 inches deep, breaking up clods as you work.
- Asparagus roots are greedy for space, so plant them 2 feet apart in rows along the border of the garden, at least 4 feet from other permanent plants, such as rhubarb or fruit trees.
- A good rule of thumb is to plant about 40 roots for a family of four—more if you plan to can or freeze some of the crop.

Onions

- For a care-free crop of onions, plant the sets in a wide row, or block and cover them immediately with a 3-inch layer of mulch. Onions will grow right up through a mulch, but most weeds will not.

Peas

- Pea pods swell before the peas inside do. Don't risk picking a panful of unfilled pods. Shell a few pods before you continue down the row. Also, try gently squeezing each pod to confirm that the peas inside are ready before picking.

Rhubarb

- Select a planting site where rhubarb hasn't been grown for four or five years. With the new location, rhubarb has a better chance of avoiding diseases. Chances of infection can be reduced further by planting rhubarb in soil with good drainage. If drainage isn't the best, try a raised bed. Edge the bed with railroad ties or cement blocks, and fill it with topsoil.

- Whether you have a raised bed or a level garden, dig a hole about a foot wide and deep enough so that the new rhubarb plant or division can be set about 2 inches below the soil surface. Allow 3 feet between the plants. Cover with topsoil (mixed with compost or peat moss). Firm the soil around the plant, but not directly over the bud.
- Don't harvest rhubarb until the second season. The second spring, you can cut it for three weeks. Wait until the third season for a full harvest.
- Rhubarb is best started by divisions. If you want divisions from an existing plant, dig deeply around the clump and lift the whole plant out of the ground. Cut through the crown between buds.

Squash

- Protect developing squash (shown above) and melons from soil-borne diseases and insect pests by perching them on a flowerpot, tin can, brick, or block of wood. Up in the air, away from the cool, damp ground, they ripen faster and develop better color and flavor.

Strawberries

- Plant strawberries in the early spring, while the weather is still cool and relatively moist. They need a sunny location with rich, well-drained soil. Space plants 8 to 10 inches apart and keep them mulched.

- There are two basic types of strawberries to choose from: June-bearers, which produce one heavy crop, and everbearers, which produce several small crops throughout the early summer and one large crop in late summer. Pick the flowers off all June-bearing varieties the first summer to allow them to build strength for a good second harvest. You can let everbearers produce a crop their first season.

- Spring is the time to loosen the mulch from your strawberries— just enough to let light reach the leaves during the first warm days. Be sure to leave the top of your cold frame ajar on warm spring days so that the plants do not overheat.

Harvest Hints

- Vegetables ripen fast during the heat of midsummer. If you're going to be away for a week's vacation, invite friends and neighbors to stop by and pick what ripens while you're gone.

- Make your garden pay for itself. In some areas, you may be able to sell your excess produce at a small stand in front of your house or at a local farmers' market.

- Pick regularly to prolong the harvest from cucumbers and summer squash. If you start letting the vegetables mature into big seedy blimps, the plants will stop producing tender new vegetables.

- Extend your season by making several small plantings of beans (shown at right), lettuce, and other fast-growing crops a week or two apart.

- Frost is most likely when the sky is clear and the air is still and dry, with no breeze and low humidity. Under these conditions, if the temperature is already low and drops quickly at sunset, cover any tender plants.

TREES AND SHRUBS

"If I were king, every gardener who has a lawn would be required to have some Forsythia."

Writings of the Plain Dirt Gardener

Good Trees...

Trees such as white birch, flowering dogwood, and Dutch elm have all been plagued with pests and diseases in recent years. If your property has pest problems, consider planting these beautiful but tough trees as substitutes:

- Heritage river birch (*Betula nigra* 'Heritage'). Handsome white bark exfoliates and reveals multicolored inner bark.
- Giant dogwood (*Cornus controversa*). The branches in this species are layered and bear small white flowers and bright red fall foliage.
- Shademaster honey locust (*Gleditsia triacanthos* var. *inermis* 'Shademaster'). This thornless, feathery cultivar was bred as an alternative to the Dutch elm.

...and Bad

- Avoid planting the following trees near streets, drives, and pipes: ash, black locust, box elder, catalpa, hawthorn, honey locust, horse chestnut, red or silver maple, mulberry, poplar, black walnut, and willow.

Shapely Specimens

Add interest to your yard with trees whose shapes enhance their surroundings.

- Weeping trees—weeping apricot, weeping European ash, weeping beech, slender European and Young's birch, weeping boree, deodar cedar, weeping cherry, pink weeper crab apple, pendula hemlock, weeping European hornbeam, pendent silver linden, several varieties of pines, several varieties of willow, and Brewer's, Koster weeping, and blue spruce.
- Columnar trees—arborvitae, pyramidal red cedar, sentry ginkgo, 'Columnaris' and 'Fastigiata' hornbeam, blue columnar juniper, lombardy poplar, 'Fastigiata' tulip tree, sentry maple, and 'Bowhill' and 'Scanlon' red maple.
- Pyramid-shaped trees—beech, birch, black gum, cedar, hemlock, holly, larch, linden, magnolia, pine, pin oak, sorrel, spruce, and sweet gum.
- Trees with horizontal branches—Chinese chestnut, dogwood (shown above), fir, hawthorn, white and live oak, redbud, red pine, Scotch pine, silk tree, and spruce.

SELECTING A TREE

Planting a tree is a long-term decision, so invest some time in making an educated choice.

- Always consider the growth rate of a plant before you buy. Fast-growing species may grow too quickly and have to be replaced in just a few years. If you want your landscaping project to look more established, spend the extra money and buy a larger specimen of a slow-growing species that won't have to be replaced or pruned so frequently.
- Find out the light requirements of each tree. Sun-loving plants can survive in a shady location, but shade dwellers are not as tolerant and may die if planted in an exposed area.
- The size of your yard will dictate how large a tree it can accommodate. Knowing a tree's mature height and shape will help you pare down your list of choices. Most trees will bear crowding, as any forest proves, but not without some sacrifice of shape.
- The size and style of your house also will dictate what tree is appropriate. Lofty trees blend beautifully with two-story houses on large lots, but the horizontal branching of smaller trees mixes better with low, ranch-style homes.
- Deciduous or evergreen? Deciduous trees offer the advantage of colorful fall foliage, but if you have an aversion to raking leaves, choose an evergreen. Evergreens keep their color year-round, making them well suited for privacy screens and windbreaks.
- Unless you're willing to go to a lot of trouble and expense, choose a tree that is known for its resistance to pests and disease. Check with an expert at a local nursery or county extension office for specific recommendations in your area. Plant a variety of trees so if disease or pests strike, they won't wipe out your entire landscape.

The Right Site

No matter which tree you choose, locate it where you'll benefit from it the most.

Getting Your Bearings

Evergreens planted on the north and west sides of your house will block winter winds and reduce heating costs. Deciduous trees planted on the south side will shade your home in the summer and let in warm sunlight in the winter.

Too Close for Comfort

Place an ornamental tree at least 15 feet from a house, a shade tree at least 25 feet. As the tree matures, it needs adequate space so that it won't grow against the building.

Living with Litter

Most trees, including horse chestnut (shown below), drop something, whether its blossoms, leaves, needles, or fruits. Locate trees where their litter won't be a nuisance.

Sun Shades

Intense afternoon sun strengthens color, so the western sides of trees often carry the most brilliant hues in early autumn—something to remember when deciding where to put deciduous trees.

Best Trees

BEST TREES

You can create an attractive landscape by choosing a variety of shade and ornamental trees. Many trees offer color and interest every season, and some are especially suited to small or shady spaces.

Best Trees for Small Yards

The following trees look good in small yards: dwarf balsam fir (*Abies balsamea* 'Nana'), Japanese maple (*Acer palmatum*), kousa dogwood (*Cornus kousa*), Asian serviceberry (*Amelanchier asiatica*), paperbark maple (*Acer griseum*), European hornbeam (*Carpinus betulus* 'Fastigiata'), showy crab apple (*Malus floribunda*), Korean mountain ash (*Sorbus alnifolia*), crape myrtle (*Lagerstroemia indica*), varnish tree (*Koelreuteria paniculata*), ornamental pear (*Pyrus calleryana*), dwarf white pine (*Pinus strobus* 'Nana'), and Hinoki false cypress (*Chamaecyparis obtusa*).

Best Trees for Shade Plants

These trees combine large canopies with deep taproots, creating ideal conditions for growing understory plants in shade. They include the following: bitternut hickory (*Carya cordiformis*), common hackberry (*Celtis occidentalis* 'Prairie Prince'), white oak (*Quercus alba*), American linden (*Tilia americana*), and Japanese zelkova (*Zelkova serrata* 'Village Green').

Best Fast-Growing Trees

Quick-growing trees include acacia, alder, black locust, catalpa, Siberian elm, Empress tree, eucalyptus, poplar, silk tree, Chinese tallow, and willow. Quick-growing trees will give you a mature-looking landscape sooner, but they also tend to be weak-wooded.

Best Trees for Fragrance

Trees that offer fragrant flowers or foliage include acacia, arborvitae, bayberry, black locust, cedar, crab apple, eucalyptus, fringe tree, fruit trees, hemlock, katsure tree, littleleaf linden, magnolia, amur maple, pine, Russian olive, silk tree, silver-bell, sorrel, and yellowwood.

Best Trees for Fruits and Berries

Fall is the time for fruits and berries. They often hang on well into winter and provide color against a snowy landscape. Select trees such as dogwood, hawthorn, Russian olive, holly, flowering crab, sourwood, goldenrain tree, and mountain ash.

Crab Apple

Magnolia

Best Evergreens with Unusual Foliage

Many evergreens have unusual foliage effects.

❧ Golden foliage—*Cupressus macrocarpa* 'Goldcrest,' Hinoki false cypress (*Chamaecyparis obtusa* 'Crippsii'), English yew (*Taxus baccata* 'Aurea'), and Nordmann fir (*Abies nordmanniana* 'Golden Spreader').

❧ Blue foliage—Blue Atlas cedar (*Cedrus atlantica* 'Glauca'), blue spruce (*Picea pungens* var. *glauca*), and Colorado spruce (*Picea pungens* 'Koster').

❧ Drooping branches—Brewer's spruce (*Picea brewerana*), American arbovitae (*Thuja occidentalis* 'Pendula'), and Canada hemlock (*Tsuga canadensis* 'Sargenti').

Best Spring-Blooming Trees

Favorite trees that bloom in spring include redbud, dogwood, pear, flowering crab, acacia, horse chestnut, hawthorn, and magnolia. Fruit trees, including apple, peach, pear, cherry, and plum, will add colorful charm.

Best Summer-Blooming Trees

Brighten the long, hot days of summer with such spectacular summer-flowering species as crape myrtle, golden-rain tree, golden-chain tree, stewartia, silk tree, Japanese tree lilac, and catalpa.

Best Trees for Fall Color

Many trees have breathtaking fall color.

❧ Yellow and gold: ash, beech, birch, butternut, ginkgo, hickory, honey locust, linden, sugar maple, pecan, poplar, tulip tree, and walnut.

❧ Red tones: dogwood, hawthorn, red maple, oak, sour gum, sourwood, or sweet gum.

❧ Bright orange: yellowwood, Ohio buckeye, and paperbark maple.

Best Trees for Winter Interest

The pageantry of trees doesn't have to close down for the season when winter arrives. You can add interest to a dreary landscape with colorful or patterned bark or an unusual trunk shape. Beautiful bark is found on crape myrtle, birch, beech, sweet gum, sycamore, willow, cherry, and eucalyptus. Trees with attractive silhouettes include weeping cherry or birch, crape myrtle, katsura tree, dogwood, magnolia, poplar, selkova tree, and tulip tree. Evergreens add color to a snowy yard.

Redbud

Ginkgo

Best Shrubs

BEST SHRUBS

Like trees, shrubs provide year-long color through fragrant blooms and changing foliage.

Best Shrubs for City Gardens

In the city, choose shrubs that can handle pollution as well as poor soil and reduced light and air circulation. Possibilities include flowering quince (*Chaenomeles speciosa*), Tartarian dogwood (*Cornus alba*), forsythia, common witch hazel (*Hamamelis virginiana*), rose-of-Sharon (*Hibiscus syriacus*), hydrangea, St.-John's-wort (*Hypericum*), Japanese holly (*Ilex crenata*), juniper, Japanese kerria (*Kerria japonica*), privet (*Ligustrum*), star magnolia (*Magnolia stellata*), Oregon grape (*Mahonia aquifolium*), shrubby cinquefoil (*Potentilla fruticosa*), firethorn (*Pyracantha coccinea*), sumac (*Rhus*), spirea, and English and Japanese yew (*Taxus baccata* and *Taxus cuspidata*).

Best Shrubs for Quick Screens

Shrubs that grow quickly include beautybush, eleagnus, euonymus, forsythia, honeysuckle, mock orange, privet, and arrowwood, nannyberry, and siebold viburnum.

Best Shrubs for Fragrance

Shrubs with fragrant flowers or foliage include azalea hybrids, bayberry, boxwood, butterfly bush, clethra, honeysuckle, lilac, privet, rhododendron hybrids, rose, and Korean spice viburnum.

Best Spring-Flowering Shrubs

Shrubs that produce lovely flowers in spring include andromeda, Korean azalea, barberry, bayberry, cinquefoil, forsythia, dwarf fruit, honeysuckle, kerria, lilac, pussy willow, rhododendron, spirea, and viburnum.

Best Summer-Flowering Shrubs

Shrubs that produce beautiful flowers in summer include arrowwood, flame azalea, butterfly bush, crape myrtle, peegee hydrangea, leucothoe, mock orange, mountain laurel, privet, rose, rose-of-Sharon, and 'Anthony Waterer' spirea.

Best Fruiting Shrubs

Shrubs and dwarf trees that produce fruit include almond, apple, apricot, blueberry, bush cherry, Surinam cherry, dwarf citrus, currant, gooseberry, pineapple guava, nectarine, peach, pear, bush plum, natal plum, pomegranate, quince, and rose (hips).

Hydrangea

Viburnum

Best Prune-Free Shrubs

Shrubs that look wonderful with little or no pruning include:

•Glossy abelia (*Abelia* x *grandiflora*), with white, funnel-shaped flowers that last all summer

•Slender deutzia (*Deutzia gracilis* 'Nikko'), a compact shrub with many white flowers in May

•Rose-of-Sharon (*Hibiscus syriacus* 'Diana'), with large, lustrous, white flowers last from summer into fall

•Oakleaf hydrangea (*Hydrangea quercifolia*), with early summer cones of white flowers that age to pink by late summer

•Mountain laurel (*Kalmia latifoli*a), with beautiful white, pink, or red spring flowers

•Japanese andromeda (*Pieris japonica*), an evergreen shrub with early spring flowers that resemble clusters of lily-of-the-valley.

Best Small Evergreens

Small evergreen shrubs provide structure and interest in the shade garden throughout the year. The yellow-flowered shrubby St.-John's-wort (*Hypericum prolificum*), the dark-pink-blossomed mountain laurel (*Kalmia latifolia* 'Elf'), and dwarf Japanese hollies (*Ilex crenata* 'Helleri' and 'Tiny Tim') require little care.

SHRUB SHAPES

■ Shrubs with arching branches include beautybush, butterfly bush, lilac daphne, slender deutzia, forsythia, and spirea.

■ Erect shrubs include highbush cranberry, red-osier dogwood, hibiscus, common lilac (shown below), and lemoine mock orange.

■ Rounded shrubs include hydrangea, kerria, Persian lilac, flowering quince, weigela, and witch hazel.

■ Spreading shrubs include spreading cotoneaster, sargent crab apple, dwarf ninebark, Japanese quince, staghorn sumac, and fragrant viburnum.

Rose-of-Sharon

Care and Maintenance of Your Trees and Shrubs

Make the most of your landscape investment by following these guidelines for strong, healthy trees and shrubs.

- To eliminate unwanted grass around newly planted trees and shrubs, put down a ¼-inch layer of newspaper before placing the mulch around the base of the plants.

- Reduce moisture loss around a newly planted tree by applying a layer of mulch 2 to 3 inches thick. Use semi-decayed wood chips, pine bark, well-decayed manure, peat moss, or leaf mold. Keep mulch away from the trunk to reduce damage caused by rodents and decay.

- Stake a new tree or shrub for a year or two until the roots are sufficiently well established to anchor the plant without assistance. Without this reinforcement, strong winds can cause the balled root to rotate like a ball-and-socket joint, breaking off fragile, newly developed roots.

- If you're thinking of moving a tree, keep this in mind: You can move trees shorter than 6 feet and with trunks less than 1 inch in diameter. Larger trees should be transplanted by professionals.

- A dose of vitamin B at planting helps a tree overcome the shock of being moved. Vitamin B for plants is available at garden centers. Follow the package directions for use.

- Wait a year after planting before fertilizing trees and shrubs. Adding fertilizer to the soil mix or the planting area after installing shrubs or trees may harm, rather than help, your newly established plants. Fertilizer harms new woody plants by burning tender root tips and by stimulating rapid growth, which puts pressure on root systems to provide nutrients to the plants while adapting to new surroundings.

- Prune the branches off your used Christmas tree, and lay the cuttings over tender low-growing shrubs. The cut branches will help insulate the shrubs from the cold and drying winter winds.

- The position of branches does not change as a tree matures—a branch that is now a few feet off the ground will always be at about the same height. Prune low branches on mature trees that shade the grass and make mowing difficult.

Planting for Proper Performance

■ Spring and fall are both good times to plant a flowering tree. However, fall is a poor time to transplant trees with thin bark, such as beech, birch, dogwood, linden, magnolia, sweetgum, and tulip tree.

■ When you dig the planting hole for a shrub, make refilling the hole easier. Put a tarp or piece of plastic next to where you'll dig the hole, then place the soil on it.

■ When you plant a balled-and-burlapped tree, dig a hole that's at least 1 foot larger in diameter and 6 inches deeper than the size of the tree's root ball. Set the tree into the hole so that it sits at the same depth that it grew in the nursery. Then roll back the burlap, but don't unwrap the ball completely.

■ Many shrubs are sold through the growing season in heavy plastic containers. Slit the containers just before you are ready to plant and gently remove the shrub, soil and all.

TREE TROUBLESHOOTING

Expert Diagnosis

Experienced staff at nurseries and your local county cooperative extension agents can help accurately diagnose both insect problems and diseases in trees. Before you spray an all-purpose poison, learn exactly what the trouble is, and then explore possible nontoxic solutions. Use poisons only with discretion and in moderation.

Treating Tree Wounds

Don't apply paint, shellac, or asphalt to tree wounds; it can cause problems. The coating eventually will crack and allow moisture to accumulate underneath, creating an ideal environment for rot.

Collision Insurance

Lawn mowers and string trimmers save lots of time when it comes to cleaning up your yard. If these tools are used improperly, however, they can cause lower-trunk injuries when their blades or nylon whips tear into the bark of trees. Avoid contact with trees when using these types of power equipment.

DANGER ZONE

Go ahead and enjoy the beauty of these shrubs, but watch out for their toxic parts: azalea (all parts), black locust (seeds, sprouts, and foliage), cherry (seeds), chokeberry (leaves, stems, bark, and seeds), daphne (berries and leaves), elderberry (all parts), golden-chain (seeds and pods), holly (berries), hydrangea (leaves and buds), jasmine (berries), magnolia (flower), oleander (bark and leaves), peach (leaves and seeds), privet (leaves and seeds), wisteria (pods and seeds), and yew (all parts).

Clip Tips

Some trees and shrubs have remarkable regenerative powers. For example, large eucalyptus trees will sprout even when cut to the ground, and overgrown box, holly, and yew hedges can be regenerated by cutting them back to bare stumps.

Most plants, however, need some foliage to transform the light and air into life-sustaining nutrients. The following are handy guidelines for proper pruning of your trees and shrubs.

Thinning

This method involves removing one or more of the old limbs at the base of the shrub. Rejuvenate an old shrub over a three-year period by cutting out about a third of the oldest canes annually.

Removing Suckers

Shrubs such as lilac and flowering almond put out numerous sucker growths from the roots. To keep the plants in bounds, cut off these suckers by digging soil away and slicing them off flush with the root.

Pruning Evergreens

Your objective? To create a natural, soft appearance that strikes a happy medium between forest-primeval shagginess and fresh-from-the-barbershop nakedness. Prune evergreens in late spring or early summer after the first burst of heavy growth, and give them a light touch-up trim in late summer so they will look shapely through winter.

Shearing Narrow-Leaved Evergreens

To prevent temporary browning on the cut ends, shear narrow-leaved evergreens, such as balsam fir, yew, and hemlock when they are wet. Choose a time after a rain or early in the morning, when the trees are still covered with dew.

Head 'em Back

Prune spring-flowering shrubs, such as mock orange, forsythia (shown at right), and lilac, immediately after flowering. Prune summer-flowering shrubs, such as kerria, rose-of-Sharon, and honeysuckle, in early spring.

HEAD 'EM BACK HARD

Shrubs with numerous twiggy branches, such as common spirea, flowering quince, and beautybush, benefit from heavy pruning deep into the crown. Remove about one-fourth of the branches yearly by cutting back half their length.

Cut to the Quick

For peak performance, some shrubs must be cut back almost to the ground level. For example, to produce big flowers on Snowhill hydrangea, cut just above the fourth bud joint above the soil. On peegee hydrangea, make cuts just above the second bud on last year's growth. Cut red-osier and golden-twig dogwood to 14-inch stubs.

Hiring a Professional

Many tree-pruning jobs can be done by the home gardener. However, it's wise to turn to a professional when the tree is very tall, the canopy is broad, or there are a lot of dangerous dead limbs.

Professionals have special equipment, such as spiked shores and safety belts, to get high into the tree safely. As needed, they also will bring industrial equipment, such as a cherry picker, to prune the crown into a symmetrical, graceful form.

Find out what approach each professional takes, then choose someone who understands how to enhance your tree's natural form. Over the years, the difference in the tree's overall appearance will be enormous.

HEDGE KNOW-HOW

■ Shrubs planted in a staggered row create a thick screen faster than a straight row. This system is usually recommended for informal, unsheared hedges. Use a taut string to guide you.

■ Prune all newly planted hedge plants. Remove three-fourths of the top growth if the hedge is to be formal; one-half for informal. Shear evergreens only enough to make them uniform.

■ To ensure a straight cut along the length of a hedge, put a stake in the ground at each end, then run a length of line between the two at the desired height (making sure the line is level).

■ Plastic sheeting can help keep weeds under control. When planting a formal hedge, lay plastic along the string line. Cut holes as needed and insert the plants.

Easy Espalier

To save time when creating an espalier, choose a tree such as pear (shown at right) that already has branches that fit your espalier design. If the ideal tree isn't available, begin with a year-old unbranched "whip."

Use young, supple branches that can take the severe bending without damage. Tie them firmly, but not so tightly that the branch is constricted. Check periodically to make sure the branch has not outgrown its tie.

Once the final size and form are achieved, continue to prune espaliered trees several times during the summer to keep the shape tight and encourage good fruit production.

THEME GARDENS

*"The secret of a healthy rose is to spray ahead of danger.
You can kill bugs after they show up but diseases must be prevented."*

Writings of the Plain Dirt Gardener

THE ROSE GARDEN

Proper Placement of Roses

By finding the perfect spot for roses, you can help ensure healthy blooming plants.

❧ To get roses off to a good start, plant them in a well-drained location where they will receive at least six hours of sunlight a day. If you have a choice between morning and afternoon sun, choose morning so the dew on the leaves will dry sooner, reducing the threat of powdery mildew or black-spot disease.

❧ Every yard has an eyesore. Use roses to camouflage trash cans, sheds, and compost areas.

❧ Never plant roses where their roots will have to compete with roots from other shrubs and trees for food and water. Windy areas also should be avoided, because high winds can destroy open flowers.

Taking Root

These steps will give roses a good start.

■ After you buy roses, soak the roots in a pail of water overnight before planting them. If you can't plant them the next day, pack the roots with wet moss or newspaper, and store the bushes in a cool, dark place. Plant them as soon as you can.

■ Before you plant a rose, locate the bud union—the point where the rose was grafted to the understock. It should be placed just above ground level after planting.

■ To plant a rose properly, dig a hole larger than the root system of the rosebush and mold loose soil into a cone in the center. Spread the roots of the rose over and around the cone, being careful not to bunch too many roots. Prune back any roots that are broken or excessively long. After the roots are arranged, fill the hole with a soil/compost mixture. Pour water over the filled hole and gently rock the rose back and forth and up and down. This will settle the soil and eliminate air pockets.

Maintaining Healthy Roses

❧ Once a rose is established, cover the ground around the base of the plant with a 2- to 3-inch mulch of straw, bark chips, pine needles, sawdust, or grass clippings.

❧ Loosen the ground around roses by lightly raking it on a regular basis. Water roses heavily about once a week in dry weather, but don't sprinkle them in the evening. Feed them liquid manure, if possible, although they will get along without it. When feeding roses, see that the soil is thoroughly watered beforehand, and go easy on feeding weaker plants.

❧ To prevent rose diseases such as black-spot or mildew, spray or dust rose foliage regularly. To control aphids, Japanese beetles, and other pests, treat them as they appear.

MAKING THE CUT

When cutting fresh flowers, make the cuts at 45-degree angles above strong, five-leaflet leaves. Be sure to leave at least two sets of leaves on each cane to maintain plant vigor. On new plants, leave as much of the cane as possible.

Cold-Weather Care

During the deep freeze of winter, warm your roses with these simple hints.

Winter Blanket

Give roses an insulating blanket of mulch for their winter nap. Move container-grown roses to a garage or porch, and cover the crowns with straw.

Snow Cones

In the coldest parts of the country, protect roses with plastic-foam cones. Wait until the ground freezes before covering the plants. Most roses will need heavy pruning to fit under the cones. Remove the covers on warm winter days to keep excess heat from stimulating plant growth too early.

THE WATER GARDEN

Getting Your Water Wings

Follow these basic guidelines to add the beauty and tranquility of water to your garden space.

- Any watertight container can become home to a water garden. For in-ground ponds, you have three basic choices: concrete-lined, plastic- or PVC-lined, or a pre-formed fiberglass pool shell.

- A water garden can be as simple as a halved barrel with a single water lily, or as elaborate as an in-ground pool teeming with flowers, foliage, fish, and fountains. Keep in mind, however, that as a pond gets smaller, the ecological balance between plants, water, fish, and other creatures is actually more difficult to maintain. Algae can build up, and the water garden is more affected by pollutants and temperature changes.

- Place a water garden where it will receive at least five hours of sun a day and be clear of trees. It also should be convenient to a garden hose. For pools that need pumps, lights, or a heater, an outdoor electric outlet should be within reach.

Seasonal Care

Simple maintenance will help you enjoy your water garden in all seasons.

Summertime Dos

During the summer months, maintain a water garden by pruning vigorous growers and picking off dead flowers and leaves. Remove surface scum with a screen-skimmer or by running a piece of newspaper across the water surface. Inspect the plants and remove those that are choking out others.

Cold-Weather Alert

In winter, hardy water lilies and lotus can stay in the water garden if their roots are not allowed to freeze. In areas where the mercury drops below zero, add a floating heater to keep the water from freezing.

Water Flora and Fauna

Prevent murky water by using a circulating pump and including the right plants and animals in your water garden.

Water Grasses

When planting grasses or grasslike plants in pots to sink into a pail of water or a pool or pond, don't use peat moss or a peat-based potting mix. Peaty mixes tend to float out of the pots when you set them in the water. A mix of builder's sand and potting soil will stay in place better. Also, before you submerge a water lily container, poke fertilizer tablets into the soil.

Oxygen-Adding Plants

After the spring sunshine has warmed your pool, get ready to plant your water garden. Establish oxygenating plants before you add them or fish to your pond. These plants have the major role of keeping the water clear by competing for the same food and light as algae. They also provide oxygen, food, hiding places, and egg-laying sites for fish. Start out with water milfoil or water weed.

Bog Plants

If your water garden is at ground level, add bog plants to the wet area around the edges of the pond. These plants include water canna, iris, water poppies, and pickerel weeds.

Floating Plants

It doesn't get any easier than this: Set floating plants on the surface of the water. Floating plants include water chestnut, water hyacinth, and water lettuce.

Water Lilies

It's generally safe to set out tender water lilies (shown below right) by mid-May. A 15-inch-square, 1-foot-deep mesh basket is usually right for each plant. Fill the box with garden loam and cover it with a thin layer of sand or small pebbles to keep the box from muddying the water.

Fish

Select a balance of ornamental fish (goldfish and koi), algae-eating snails, turtles, tadpoles, and frogs (shown below left). If you have a small pond, don't overcrowd your fish or they could die from lack of oxygen.

REGIONAL FAVORITES

Plant wildflowers native to your own area of the country.

- *Pacific Northwest.* California poppy, calliopsis, Chinese-houses, coreopsis, five-spot, gumbo lily, mountain phlox, prairie coneflower, and sneezeweed.

- *Southwest.* California poppy, calliopsis, Chinese-houses, coneflower, coreopsis, gumbo lily, Indian blanket (perennial), prairie coneflower, and tahoka daisy.

- *Northeast.* Black-eyed Susan, butterfly weed, calliopsis, coreopsis, evening primrose, Indian blanket, New England aster, oxeye daisy, purple coneflower (shown below), and swamp sunflower.

- *Midwest.* Black-eyed Susan, butterfly weed, coreopsis, Indian blanket, prairie coneflower, sneezeweed, sundrops, sunflower, and swamp sunflower.

- *Southeast.* Bachelor's buttons, black-eyed Susan, butterfly weed, calliopsis, coneflower, coreopsis, Indian blanket, oxeye daisy, purple coneflower (shown below), and Texas plume.

Meadow-Garden Maintenance

Cut a meadow at least once a year, usually at the end of the growing season after the plants have set seed. Cut to a height of 4 to 6 inches. When cutting grasses, be sure to match the mower to the job. Lawn mowers are a poor—and sometimes dangerous—tool to cut most field grasses. For cutting small fields yearly, use a hand scythe or swing blade on a grass edger. Keep all blades used for cutting grasses as sharp as possible.

SOWING THE SEEDS

Create Your Own Seed Mix

Select a blend of annuals, perennials, and biennials that will grow well in your area. For successive bloom, include species that bloom in the spring, summer, and fall. The number of seeds you need depends on the type of mixture you have and germination rates. A general rule is to use 6 to 8 pounds of seed per acre.

Broadcast Planting

To get the best coverage, mix wildflower seeds with equal amounts of dry sand or sawdust. Broadcast one portion of the seed-sand mixture over the entire area by hand or with a mechanical seed spreader. Then rake to barely cover the seeds with soil and tamp down lightly. Water the seed beds until the plants are established.

TAMING WILDFLOWERS

Simple steps will yield bountiful results.

Select the Site

Pick an area that receives at least six to eight hours of sunshine a day. Most meadow plants will survive in infertile soils, but good drainage is important. If your soil is heavy with clay or in an area that drains poorly, add organic matter to improve drainage.

Work the Soil

Wildflowers need loose soil in order to grow, so till the area to a depth of 6 to 8 inches. In doing so, you'll also pull up any weed seeds that have been lying dormant and that will compete with your wildflowers. You can eliminate weeds with an herbicide after they begin to grow, but wait two weeks before you plant wildflower seeds.

They're a Natural

It's best to plant only those wildflower species, such as black-eyed Susan (*Rudbeckia hirta,* shown below), that are native to your part of the country. After all, these plants are already adapted to your specific growing conditions. When buying a wildflower seed mixture, choose one that is designed for your area. Avoid 'all America' or general meadow mixtures. You'll be wasting your money on the seeds that aren't native to your area.

Wildflowers for Woodlands

Good plants for woodland shade settings abound.

❧ Goatsbeard (*Aruncus dioicus*), 6-foot plants with compound leaves and showy plumes of tiny white flowers.
❧ Fairy-candles (*Cimicifuga americana*), which have good foliage and slender wands of tiny white flowers up to 4 feet tall.
❧ Bunchberry (*Cornus canadensis*), with creamy white petals (*really bracts*) followed by red berries.
❧ White snakeroot (*Eupatorium rugosum*), with white powder-puff flowers on top of 3-foot stems.
❧ Wake-robin (*Trillium grandiflorum*), which bears showy three-petaled white flowers that turn deep pink with age on 14-inch stems.

Dozens of fern species also are at home in a woodland garden—hayscented fern (*Dennstaedtia punctilobula*), beautiful but spreads aggressively; ostrich fern (*Matteuccia pensylvanica*), tall and plumed; maidenhair fern (*Adiantum pedatum*); maidenhair speenwort (*Asplenium trichomanes*); lady fern (*Athyrium filix-femina*); sensitive fern (*Onoclea sensibilis*); interrupted fern (*Osmunda claytoniana*); and Christmas fern (*Plystichum acrostichoides*), an evergreen that reaches 12½ feet tall.

THE WILDLIFE GARDEN

Drawing a Crowd

Before you plan your wildlife garden, do some research. Learn about local plants you can grow that are attractive to wildlife. Check with local conservation groups to determine the species in your area and their food and cover requirements.

Butterflies

- Tempt butterflies such as Tiger Swallowtails (shown below) with a mass planting of white or pink coneflower. These hardy perennials bloom all summer long. Another butterfly favorite is tithonia, sometimes called Mexican sunflower, which produces bright orange flowers.
- Monarch butterflies will feast on almost any colorful bloom. Their young, however, eat only milkweed plants. During migration, monarch butterflies depend on fall-blooming flowers such as New England asters for nourishment during their long trek south.
- You'll attract more butterflies to your garden if you plant their favorite flowers in drifts or clumps. Zinnias, for example, are a preferred food for many butterfly species, especially when the flowers are crowded together in a large mass.

Toads

- Toads are often a gardener's best friend. From spring through fall, they will consume thousands of insects and other pests, including cutworms, beetles, caterpillars, and slugs. Just give them a shallow pan of water in a shady spot to keep them settled on your property.

Birds and Bees

- Your garden will attract its share of birds if it offers plenty of natural food, suitable cover for safe nesting and perching, and fresh water. Making your garden attractive to birds makes sense. In addition to contributing beauty and music, birds consume thousands of insects and garden pests.
- Most native plants attract more birds than do exotic or rare plants. Birds' favorite plants are viburnum, holly, grape, bayberry, bittersweet, hawthorn, blueberry, shadbush or serviceberry, chokeberry, dogwood, elderberry, and honeysuckle. Other popular plants include pyracantha, crab apple, Russian olive, autumn olive, mountain ash, and cherry.
- Several types of trees are attractive to birds—pine, spruce, oak, maple, birch, and beech, among others.
- Put trumpet vine on the menu if you want to attract hummingbirds and bumblebees. The vines flower from June to August.

Bugs

- Plant a mix of flowers for a spring-to-fall supply of blooms. Because different insects are attracted to different hues, plant a broad range of flower colors. Include fragrant flowers and herbs in your garden plan. Always plant in mass, not just two or three species.
- Insects love both the wild and cultivated forms of yarrow. Be sure to set out extra plants for indoor bouquets.

CREATURE FEATURES

To attract wildlife to your garden, simply. . .

Go Wild!

You'll attract more wildlife if you aren't too tidy. Let the edges of your property go wild with native vegetation. Learn to tolerate a few weeds like dandelion, thistle, and clover as well.

Enhance the Habitat

The greater number of places and the more diversity you offer wildlife, the greater number and diversity of creatures you'll attract. If you have enough space, create a variety of habitats, such as ponds, meadows, and flower gardens.

ENVIRONMENTAL PROTECTION

Creatures need protection from fierce weather. You can create an appealing habitat for small mammals, such as chipmunks, rabbits, raccoons, skunks, or opossums, by piling up brush or boulders, perhaps burying PVC pipe at the bottom. Leave a dead tree alone, unless it's posing a risk; it will provide a home for birds and animals, plus provide an insect banquet for birds.

INDEX